Tongues of Fire

Tongues of Fire

Theological Reflections on Pentecost

Paul O. Ingram

CASCADE *Books* • Eugene, Oregon

TONGUES OF FIRE
Theological Reflections on Pentecost

Copyright © 2019 Paul O. Ingram. All rights reserved. Except for brief quotations in critical publications or reviews, no part of this book may be reproduced in any manner without prior written permission from the publisher. Write: Permissions, Wipf and Stock Publishers, 199 W. 8th Ave., Suite 3, Eugene, OR 97401.

Cascade Books
An Imprint of Wipf and Stock Publishers
199 W. 8th Ave., Suite 3
Eugene, OR 97401

www.wipfandstock.com

PAPERBACK ISBN: 978-1-5326-8258-2
HARDCOVER ISBN: 978-1-5326-8259-9
EBOOK ISBN: 978-1-5326-8260-5

Cataloguing-in-Publication data:

Names: Ingram, Paul O., author.

Title: Tongues of fire : theological reflections on Pentecost / Paul O. Ingram.

Description: Eugene, OR: Cascade Books, 2019. | Includes bibliographical references.

Identifiers: ISBN 978-1-5326-8258-2 (paperback). | ISBN 978-1-5326-8259-9 (hardcover). | ISBN 978-1-5326-8260-5 (ebook).

Subjects: LCSH: Theology. | Holy Spirit.

Classification: BT123 I54 2019 (print). | BT123 (ebook).

Scripture quotations are taken from New Revised Standard Version Bible, copyright © 1989 National Council of the Churches of Christ in the United States of America. Used by permission. All rights reserved worldwide.

Manufactured in the U.S.A.　　　　　　　　　　　　　　　09/30/19

Contents

Preface | vii

1. A Reflection on Pentecost | 1
2. A Reflection on the Trinity | 5
3. Bread Is Life | 11
4. When Law and Compassion Conflict | 18
5. The Bloody Truth | 23
6. Jesus and James on "True Religion" | 26
7. A Woman of Faith | 30
8. Who Did the Historical Jesus Say He was? | 34
9. The Death of Jesus and the Future of Violence | 40
10. A Theological Hodgepodge | 47
11. The Politics of Grace | 53
12. The Rich Man | 59
13. James and John Make a Request | 63
14. Blind Bartimaeus | 69
15. Reformation Day | 73
16. All Saints' and Sinners' Day | 79
17. The Prophetic Widow | 84
18. Whom Shall We Trust? | 88
19. "What is Truth?" | 94
20. An Epilogue in Process | 98

Bibliography | 103

Preface

Originally, "Pentecost" referred to the Jewish feast of Weeks, that is, Shau'ot, held fifty days (hence the name) after Passover. In Christian use, "Pentecost" specifically refers to an event when, according to the account in Acts 2, the Holy Spirit descended on the early Christian community in Jerusalem "with the noise of a strong driving wind" and "tongues of fire," so that the people gathered began to speak in foreign languages that everyone present understood. Pentecost is celebrated on the first Sunday after Easter. The Season after Pentecost, also called Ordinary Time, begins the day after Pentecost and ends on the day before the First Sunday of Advent. It may include twenty-three to twenty-eight Sundays, depending on the date of Easter. Furthermore, there are three liturgical "seasons of Pentecost" labeled A, B, and C. In each of these "seasons," different Gospel texts are emphasized: Matthew in season A, Mark in season B, and Luke in season C. The twenty essays in this book are theological reflections on selected Sunday texts for Pentecost in season B.

In the liturgical calendar, the period from Pentecost Sunday until the last Sunday of Pentecost is the longest period of the church's liturgical calendar. I focused on the Season B texts because: (1) the primary gospel texts are those in Mark, which is oldest of the three synoptic gospels dating shortly after 70 CE and closest to the events surrounding the life of the historical Jesus; (2) but since other biblical texts from the Tanak and the epistles are also read as lessons leading up the gospel text for each Sunday, I have included commentary and interpretation on these texts as well; and (3) as a point of confession, Mark's gospel in my favorite because the unknown author of Mark is starkly straightforward in his portrayal of the historical Jesus's journey to his death in Jerusalem, the reasons behind his death, and how the terrible tragedy of his crucifixion transformed the historical Jesus into the Christ of faith.

Mark's audience was a collection of "Jewish" followers of the Christian Way who, along with their Jewish brothers and sisters, were undergoing extremely harsh persecution by the Romans during Rome's invasion of Palestine and the destruction of the Jerusalem Temple in 70 CE. Both Israelite and the Judahite followers of the Jesus Way experienced terrible suffering. Mark's message to these communities was to not lose hope, but rather to keep on keeping on following the Jesus Way. God is active in historical events and in the lives of faithful human beings because, as with the historical Jesus confessed to be the Christ of faith, faithful lives might end on a cross, but this is not the final ending.

Although each essay is focused on a particular gospel text, mostly from Mark, specific texts from the Tanak, the Psalms, the Prophets, Paul's epistles, and post-Pauline epistles are listed at the beginning of each essay. Reading these texts before reading a specific essay will, hopefully, provide a context for deeper understanding the content of each essay. Finally, while these collected essays are not heavily footnoted, a selected bibliography is included of texts and essays that have deeply influenced each essay.

I also wish to express my gratitude to K. C. Hanson and his colleagues at Cascade Books / Wipf and Stock Publishers for his and their support of my work over more years than I like to remember. Finally, this collection of essays is dedicated to Pastors John and Joan Beck and the community of Pointe of Grace Lutheran Church in Mukilteo, Washington.

— 1 —

A Reflection on Pentecost

Acts 2:1–21
Psalm 104:24–34, 35b
Romans 8:22–27
John 15:26–27; 16:4–15

Pentecost celebrates the countless expressions of God's love and wisdom. Like a skilled dancer, God's Holy Spirit moves through all creation bringing forth life and love and inspiration. Fire and wind are everywhere. Inspiration and revelation are just a moment away and can come either by surprise or as a result of the interplay between God's wisdom and our intentional spiritual practices. The Spirit blows where it wills, in all directions, embracing all life, human and nonhuman.

In other words, Pentecost is about God's omnipresence, which I interpret through the categories of Whiteheadian process theology as God's ever present "initial aim" that all things and events at every moment of space-time achieve the maximum self-fulfillment of which they are capable. Intentionally conforming our "subjective" aims for our own fulfillment in harmony with God's initial aim for us, as exemplified by the historical Jesus, is the call of Pentecost. Omnipresence is an all or nothing deal. God can't be a little omnipresent. Either God is present in, with, and under everything and event since the beginning of creation—what theologians and philosophers call "panentheism"—or omnipresence makes no sense. Nor is the God of Tanak and the New Testament—and process theology—present in a homogenous or passive manner in human life and in the evolutionary process happening throughout the universe. As I write these words, God is an active, personal, intimate, and vision-oriented presence moving always and everywhere in the direction of Shalom, of interdependent wholeness and peace. God's spirit touches every life, opening us toward communion, inspiration, and creation. Moreover, if God's aim is, as Jesus proclaimed, "abundant life," then every expression of God's presence lures us toward the personal and corporate wholeness appropriate to our context and the greater good of humans and non-humans alike. The Spirit may challenge and rebuke, but its intention is always the creation of just, compassionate community, as Micah 6:8 has it.

This is the point of the passage from Romans 8 about the universality of divine revelation. The groans of the spirit move through all creation—including the non-human world as well as human life. The sighs of creation are too deep for words, yet they move through the unconscious and "intercede" on our behalf and give us guidance in every moment of life—if we pay attention. God aims all things toward the good within us and around us, meaning the maximum intensity of beauty and wholeness—that joins our evolution with the evolution of the universe. These aims are not all-determining but rather all-orienting in the context of the many factors that influence each moment of experience. Another way of expressing this is that the inspiration of the Holy Spirit is not occasional nor is it parochial, but all encompassing, luring forth all life with visions appropriate to each individual's complexity and context. Anything touched by God, human and non-human, is of value and can be a vehicle of revelation. Awaken to divine intercession, to God's dream for you, so shouts Romans 8:22–27.

This is why one of my favorite writers, Annie Dillard, advised that we should strap on safety helmets and lash ourselves to our pews whenever we attend worship.[1] After all, worship is, in the words of Alfred North Whitehead, an "adventure" of the spirit. We claim great things in worship and should be prepared for surprise and adventure whenever we gather as a community of faith.

---

1. Dillard, *Teaching a Stone to Talk,* 40.

The living God of Pentecost calls us to expect great things—of ourselves and the creative movements of God. This adventurous Spirit was surely at work among the Pentecost Christians. They were surprised by wind, flame, and word. Pentecost joins mysticism with mission. The ecstatic experiences of Jesus' first followers—including the women following Jesus' Way—drove them into the streets to share words of graceful transformation with people of all nations. What is most exciting is that God moved through listener and speaker alike, creating a synergy of revelation and salvation. Lives were joined and transformed, despite the differences of race, language, class, and gender.

Peter's sermon, grounded in the prophetic words of Joel, describes God's embrace of all the peoples of the earth and enjoins us to cross every boundary to fulfill our role as God's partners in healing the world. A church community grounded in Pentecost goes beyond homogeneity to embrace diversity in all its many forms. God's providence encourages diversity in congregations as the foundation of spiritual growth and mission. This is what it means to be a church community founded on unity in diversity, always moving outward in ever-expanding circles of grace.

Psalm 124 complements the global experience of the Pentecost people. God's works are many and varied. God's wise *ruach*, God's "breath," moves through every creature giving life and energy, just as God's *ruach* breathed life into Adam in the creation story of Genesis 2. And John's Gospel describes the coming of an Advocate, God's Spirit whose presence will guide and sustain us. God never leaves us without wisdom—if we pay attention. There is a voice of truth in every situation. God is constantly giving us the wisdom we need in the form of possibilities to lure us forward and the energy to manifest these possibilities in our daily life.

Pentecost is visionary, but it also invites us to embrace practices for receiving the Spirit's guidance and wisdom. The Spirit is free, but often we are oblivious to it. We listen to the Spirit, as did those first Pentecost people, by personal and communal prayer and meditation. God's wisdom touches groups and persons together, and we can create an environment of receptivity when we pray and open ourselves to whatever surprises God might place in our individual and communal life. But we must be prepared to move with the Spirit, and that means mission. When we operate from a place of mission, new and more exciting missions emerge, bringing wholeness to us and to those we serve. Further, practicing Pentecost involves openness to diversity. We need to be open to the many reflections of God in the world and humankind. In other words, to the degree we think God is omnipresent, to that degree every moment can bring inspiration and invitation. Everyone, deep down, has the capacity to hear God and be a companion on the Pentecost journey, despite—and especially as a result of—their differences. We are one and many in God's ever-surprising Spirit. We need to breathe in God's spirit and make every moment a prayer and a mission.

— 2 —

A Reflection on the Trinity

Isaiah 6:6–8
Psalm 29
Romans 8:12–17
John 3:1–7

I have always been mystified by the doctrine of the Trinity. On a Trinity Sunday twenty years ago, a colleague of mine in the Department of Religion at Pacific Lutheran University asked me what I thought about the Trinity. When I said that the simplest explanation I could think of was that "the Father" referred to God and "the Son" was the historical Jesus who had surrendered his will for himself to God's will for Jesus to such a degree that in Jesus' life and death persons of faith experienced, partially at least, something of God's reality. "The Spirit," I continued "points to God's creative presence in the universe since the first moment of creation to the life, death, and resurrection of the historical Jesus two thousand years ago, to God's continuing creative activity up to the present, and in whatever the future ends up becoming."

My colleague grinned and said, "You could never be ordained in the Lutheran Church with that understanding."

"That's OK," I said, "university teaching is my calling, not ordination."

The doctrine of the Trinity is the most difficult doctrine to comprehend in the history of Christian theological reflection. There exists no explicit Trinitarian teaching in either the Tanak or the New

Testament. But the foundation for Trinitarian thinking originated in Christian reflection about the relation of the historical Jesus to God as the Jesus Way gradually separated from the Jewish Way. Just how was God experienced in the life, death, and resurrection of the historical Jesus, and how is God's presence to be comprehended after his death and resurrection? All questions with which a developing Jewish Way would not be concerned.

For first to fourth-century Christians the questions were: (1) what is the real relationship between the historical Jesus Christians confess to be the "Christ" (literally Greek for "messiah") and God; (2) what is the relationship between God, the historical Jesus, and the continuing work of God through the Holy Spirit? Debates between bishops and theologians throughout the Roman Empire were contentious and often very angry, as well as socially disruptive—something no Roman emperor would tolerate. Thus in 325, Emperor Constantine, who had converted to the Christian Way as he sought to unify the Western part of the Roman empire, called into session the Council of Nicaea. Constantine's problem was that there were so many versions of the Christian Way floating about that he wasn't sure which version should be declared the official state religion. The dominant issue was the relationship between Jesus and God. Was Jesus only a prophetic human being, or was there something divine about the historical Jesus and what was this "something?"

The question is metaphysical and the theologians at Nicaea drew upon the influential philosophical speculations of Aristotle. Aristotle wrote that a "thing" is a "formed substance." "Substance" was his name for the "stuff" that comprises all things and events, while "form" was his name for the "patterns" that substances in nature assume. Another way of saying this is that "substance" names the physical "stuff" assumed by the specific "forms" that constitute all things and events. So, for example, an apple is a formed apple-substance, while a dog is an example of stuff formed into dog, while a human being is an example of stuff formed into a human being. But no two apples are identical because the substances of apples assume a multitude of "apple-forms"; for the same reason no two dogs are alike; nor are any two human beings identical. But the formed stuff that constitutes God is unique to God and is unchanging and unmoving. God is therefore an unmoved mover, who, like a magnet, moves all things and events according to the specific formed stuff all things assume. No two things (formed matter) are alike, all moving like metallic beads around a divine electromagnet, crashing and colliding, to form the substantial things we all experience, including our own bodies.

Following the broadest outlines of Aristotle's metaphysics, the majority of the bishops and scholars attending the Council of Nicaea, led by the bishop of Alexandria, decreed that the Father (God) and the Son (the historical Jesus) are *homoousios* or the "same substance." That is the "stuff" that forms God and the "stuff" that formed the historical Jesus are identical. But the problem with this formulation is that in Aristotle's philosophy, God's substance is shaped by an unchanging, eternally divine form, while Jesus' substance is shaped by a specific human form. How, therefore, can God and the historical Jesus share the same substance, since they are shaped by two different forms?

By the Council of Constantinople (381 CE), an anti-subordinationist reading, vigorously championed by Alexandrian bishop Athanasius (d. 373) had the upper hand; *homoousios* was understood as asserting the Father and Son are not merely similar beings, but in some sense "one being." While stopping short of saying that the Holy Spirit was *homoousios* with the Father and Son, the council did say that the Holy Spirit "is worshiped and glorified together with the Father and the Son," and added in a letter accompanying their creed that the three share "a single Godhead and power and substance." Over the ensuing period the same sorts of arguments used to promote the divinity of the Son were reapplied to the Holy Spirit, and eventually inhibitions against applying *homoousios* to the Holy Spirit evaporated. God, the historical Jesus, and the Holy Spirit are embodied by one "substance" in three different forms—an application of Aristotle's metaphysics that must have made him turn over in his grave because for him, no thing (formed matter or substance) can be identical with any other thing (formed matter or substance).

The problem with the doctrine of the Trinity, at least for process theologians like me, is its incoherence because of its appropriation of the category of substance that is the physical foundation of everything that exists formed into changing actual things and events. Forms do not change, but substances do. But according to Alfred North Whitehead, the universe is an ever-changing system of impermanent and interdependent relationships between things and events. There exists no unchanging, underlying substance "formed into" things and events. Actual things—"societies" of actual occasions of experience—are always in flux, are always undergoing change guided by an actual occasion's or society of actual occasion's subjective aim to achieve its maximum self-fulfillment, but simultaneously guided by God's initial aim for that occasion of experience. Again, there is no underlying unchanging substance.

This is the main reason I find the traditional doctrine of the Trinity so incoherent. It is so counterintuitive to what the sciences have discovered about the physical realities at play in the universe, never mind that it is a doctrine whose categories are so deeply incoherent in its appropriation of Aristotle's philosophical thought. "It's a mystery you must accept on faith," I have been told on more occasions I can count, which means "faith" means believing something irrational and incoherent as the foundation of Christian faith and practice. For me, "faith" does not entail "believing" an irrational doctrine that reflects neither the physical process at play in the universe nor human experience. So how do I understand the interrelationship between God, the historical Jesus who for me is also the Christ of faith, and the Holy Spirit?

In reflecting on this question, I am theologically guided by a process worldview grounded in my understanding of Alfred North Whitehead as this has informed process theology, particularly that of John B. Cobb, Jr. Process thought focuses on the structures of experience in an ever-changing universe. There is no such thing as permanence, no such reality as substance. All things and events, in Whiteheadian categories, "actual entities

A REFLECTION ON THE TRINITY

and societies of actual entities" or "actual occasions of experience"—from subatomic particles to human beings to the universe itself—are constantly changing in relation to all that exists. This means that, for example, every human being is guided by his or her own internal "subjective aim" to achieve whatever he or she deems suitable for individual self-fulfillment in isolation from other human beings following their subjective aims for themselves. But from subatomic particles to human beings, God offers an "initial aim" to achieve the maximum intensity of beauty actual beings are capable of achieving, here "beauty" meaning an integrative wholeness greater than the sum of its parts.

All human beings follow their individual subjective aims mostly to the exclusion of other human beings and life forms with whom we share this planet. This sort of "egoism" is labeled "sin" in Christian tradition. Yet God's initial aim is always operating in all things and events. But most often our individual subjective aims for ourselves dominate our lives. Yet occasionally, some human beings subordinate their individual subjective aims to God's initial for them. Examples abound: Nelson Mandela, Mahatma Gandhi, Martin Luther King Jr., the pastors of my local Lutheran congregation, John and Joan Beck, the current Pope, Francis, several feminist theologians I know, including Marit Trelstad and Nancy Howell. But I think the historical Jesus became the Christ of faith because he completely subordinated his subjective aim for himself to God's initial aim for Jesus. Or as the Gospel of Mark has it, on the night of his betrayal in the Garden of Gethsemane, "not what I want but what you want" (Mark 14:36).

But the reality Christians name "God" cannot be confined to any single religious Way because the reality of God—that which constitutes God as God—is both unity and plurality. This is the deepest content of Christian experience symbolized by the doctrine of the Trinity. God is one and God is plural, which again, as it turns out can be conceptualized in the categories of process theology. God's "primordial nature," meaning God's self-identity through the moments of God's time, which is what God always is as God—beyond the categories of thought and always in interdependent relationship with the universe God continually creates—can be understood as the First Person of the Trinity ("the Father"). Yet the primordial nature of god is always in non-dual interdependency with the "plurality" of God's "consequent nature"—God as God mutually affects and is affected by all things and events in the universe throughout the moments of God's experience—two thousand years ago through the Second Person (the Son) and before and after the death of the historical Jesus through the Third Person (the Holy Spirit). God in God's primordial nature needs "manyness" to be God in God's consequent nature.

So even though the language here is too patriarchal and perhaps too abstract, "the Father" names God's creative presence in the world since the first moment of the Big Bang until the present and into the future as the Holy Spirit. "The Son" names God's creative encounter with humanity through the life, death, and resurrection of the historical Jesus Christians confessed to be the Christ of faith. "The Holy Spirit" names God's continuing creativity that reflects God creative work before and up to the life of Jesus and after's Jesus' death until the universe's time runs out billions of years into the future.

— 3 —

Bread Is Life

1 Kings 19:4–8
Psalm 34:1–8
Ephesians 4:25—5:2
John 6:35, 41–51

Wherever human beings evolved from wondering hunter-gathering societies to settled agricultural societies the religious significance of food evolved with them. Hunters apprehended the Sacred incarnated in the animals upon which they depended: bison, elk, deer, salmon, whales. Hunters performed rituals to thank the animals they killed along with rituals to resurrect them so that their food supply would continue. But when human beings settled down in villages, towns, and cities, the religious significance of food changed. Bread became the center of what people grew and ate. It was the source of daily life and supported whatever else people could grow or gather for food—fruits and grains of various kinds and meat from domesticated farm animals. Bread was life; without bread, there was no life, or as the Lord's Prayer has it, "Give us today our daily bread."

But along with bread, wine assumed an equal importance and religious symbolism that pointed to the Sacred reality that persons of Jesus's time named YHWH, or Adonai Elohim, or in closest English approximation, "God." Wine and bread were eaten at every meal, whether one was a peasant—as Jesus and his disciples were—or a priest, scribe, land owner, or a Roman governor named Pontius Pilate. Wine and bread were the foundation of family, social, communal, and religious life cross-culturally two thousand years ago.

So too with water, again a source sustaining life socially and individually. Wells were places for social gathering as people met each other as they brought large jugs to fill and take home for drinking, cooking, and every once in a while, for bathing. As with bread and wine, water too is life and points to God's care for all living things inhabiting this planet. And of course, there's John the Baptist pouring water over his followers in the Jordan River, including the historical Jesus, to wash away the sin of not following God's Torah or "Instructions."

Bread as life, wine as life, water as life are three interdependent themes that occur throughout the Gospel of John. John's gospel is quite different from the Synoptic Gospels—Matthew, Mark, and Luke-Acts. First of all, it is the latest of the four gospels and dates between 90–110. The author of John is unknown, but the discourses contained in this gospel seem to be concerned with issues of church verses synagogue. It is notable that in John, his "gentile" Christian community appears to define itself primarily in contrast to the Jewish Way. Though the Jesus Way started as a movement within Israelite and Judean traditions, by the year 90 it gradually separated from these traditions because of disagreements about the identity of the Messiah. For Judean and Gentile followers of the Jesus Way, the Messiah was Jesus—Jesus is the Messiah who had lived and died in Jerusalem and had been resurrected and would return to initiate a new age of justice and compassion. For followers of the Jewish Way, the Messiah would be one like David sent by God to establish a Kingdom of God centered in Jerusalem in a distant future of God's choosing.

In other words, Jesus was not the Messiah. Accordingly, the author of the Gospel of John defined his Christian community in direct opposition to the Jewish Way. Which explains the fact that the author of John blames the Judeans for Jesus's death more so than the Romans and the fact that later interpreters of John transformed John's Gospel into the most ant-Jewish text in the New

Testament. But in point of fact, Jesus was very popular with ordinary Jewish people, although not so much with the priests of the Jerusalem temple, who convinced Pontius Pilate to crucify him. "The Jews" did not kill the historical Jesus. Pontius Pilate and the Romans oppressing Judea killed Jesus.

All this being said about John's historical context, the author reflects on three themes that also run throughout the Tanak and the New Testament: (1) trust that God is doing something new, which circumstances can neither undermine nor negate; (2) submit everything, even our highest-stake issues and our most pressing concerns, to God; and (3) be less concerned about what we do and remain perceptive and open to what God is doing.

All of this sounds like good advice. But how do these three themes really sit with us? We wistfully tolerate this to-do list until something bad happens—a plane crashes, a war erupts, a toddler is diagnosed with cancer, a teenager experiences discrimination firsthand, a grandparent is stricken with Alzheimer's, a church leader crosses a boundary, a police officer unnecessarily fires his or her weapon, or a self-centered rich man who abuses women manages to get himself elected President of the United States. And then we know that God does not speak up, let alone step up. Then leaving everything up to God seems naive, if not ridiculous and we soon have had enough of such silly church talk and think we know too much for it to be true. One of my favorite mystical theologians, John of the Cross, referred to this experience as a "dark night of the soul," which Herman Melville in *Moby-Dick* called a "dark November of the soul." We've all experienced such moments, and when we do, it's very hard to "keep on keeping on," as my Hebrew Bible teacher, Willis Fisher, used to say.

Perhaps this is what happened to the crowd confronting Jesus; they knew too much for Jesus' words to ring true. When Jesus said, "I am the bread that came down from heaven" (John 6:41), the Judeans object and murmur among themselves. These are the insiders, the ones who know their history of suffering under Roman domination even as they follow God's "Instructions" in the Torah, the ones who know how God does things and how things should be done. They also know where Jesus came from. "Who does he think he is?" they mutter, "claiming to have come down from heaven? We know his family. We know he came from Nazareth, not from heaven!" (verse 42) The Judeans also know their scripture. "The bread from heaven was the manna fed to our ancestors back in the time of Moses," they correctly point out. And the Judeans know the Torah. "The LORD God said, 'I am the LORD your God; you shall have no other gods.'"

But a little knowledge can be a dangerous thing, and it can lead us to some muddleheaded conclusions. When it comes to God, we know only a little. Like all living things, the Church—and our understanding of God—continues to grow and change. And so, to know only a little while thinking the little that we know is all that there is to know, can be fatal. The unknown author of John thought the Judeans had some head knowledge about God, but they did not know enough to trust God. Thus, Jesus says to them, "Everyone who has heard and learned from the Father comes to me" (John 6:45). The Judeans knew some things, but their knowing was limited, and they let it close their ears, shut their hearts, and limit their vision. They were unable to hear and know what God was trying to show them. They had made up their minds and did not want to be confronted with what Jesus tried to teach them.

How often does that ring true for us? When are we like John's portrayal of the Judeans? What issues reveal that we know too much about the Jesus of our traditions and not enough about what God is doing now? When do we allow our knowledge of the history of the past to close our eyes to the working of God in the present? When are we looking and listening with open hearts? When are we willing to be drawn to the Bread of life, rather than put our trust in what we know? What do we do when we have known God not to speak up, let alone to step up? What do we do when leaving everything up to God seems naive, if not ridiculous? What do we do when we have had enough of silly church talk because we just know too much for it to be true?

I remember it like it was yesterday. In 1964, my last semester at the Claremont School of Theology, I was enrolled in a seminar

BREAD IS LIFE

on the eighth-century prophets—Amos, Hosea, Micah, and First Isaiah (which comprises chapters 1–39). The semester was rapidly drawing to a close as I was putting the finishing touches on a paper on Amos's "poem against the surrounding nations" in chapters 1–3 as I struggled with the Hebrew text. Furthermore, I had to turn the paper in that afternoon to a German biblical scholar who didn't accept late papers. Around 10:00 in the morning, a knock on the door of my wife's and my apartment interrupted my efforts to translate a very difficult passage in chapter 2. I was very annoyed and even more so when I opened the door and came face to face with a young woman holding her Bible in one hand and her very young daughter in the other. Here first words were, "Do you believe in the Bible?"

"Not only do I believe in the Bible, I've seen it," I answered sarcastically.

"I'd like to talk to you about the Bible," she persisted in a gentle voice.

"Ok," I replied. "Come in and let's talk." Then I opened my Greek New Testament and set it beside the Hebrew text of Amos. "Where do you want to begin?" I asked.

The young woman looked at me with sad eyes, picked up her Bible as she took her daughter's hand, and said, "I'll pray for you" as she left my apartment.

And I, feeling very smug, finished my paper, turned it in that afternoon, and received an "A" for the course.

But later that week, I began to think more seriously about what had transpired between this young Bible-and-daughter-totting-woman and me. What motivated this woman to knock on the doors of strangers to ask if they had read the Bible? This is not a particularly safe thing to do because you never know what sort of people will open the door. But nevertheless, she knocked on every door in my apartment complex as well as every door in the neighborhood, knowing that it was probable that she would be verbally abused by whoever open their doors.

Why do religious people like this young woman knock on the doors of strangers to convince them that they should accept

15

their version of Christian faith? The only answer I could come up with was that something wonderful, at least for her, must have happened. Maybe she heard some television evangelist and found the strength to get help for drug addiction. Maybe some fundamentalist preacher's sermons gave her the strength to get out of an unhealthy marriage to an abusive husband. Or maybe she found new meaning in her life that saved her from suicide. I don't know, but something wonderful must have happened to this woman to give her the courage to knock on the doors of strangers and face the likelihood of abuse. I was theologically trained. She was not. And on this basis, I treated her abusively and very unfairly because I put too much trust in what I thought I knew.

The historical Jesus Christians confess to be the Christ of Faith does not call us to abandon our knowledge and tradition as if they still cannot teach us anything. But Jesus cautions us that our knowledge will not give us absolute answers or a foolproof plan to make things right, that we should never cling to what we think we know because God rarely reassures us that our knowledge and understanding perfectly correspond to reality, "reality" meaning "the way things really are." If anything, God uses our partial knowledge to give a purpose, a journey, and a direction. Whatever the particular details of this journey are, its purpose is to draw us into life as part of God's coming reign, which human-constructed circumstances and conditions cannot undermine or negate, let alone perfectly understand. The risk of setting out on the journey, a journey that requires trusting and following God, is that, even when we think we have a map or a plan, we do not really know where we are going or where we will end up. Or to paraphrase Dietrich Bonhoeffer, "When God calls you, he calls you to your death." Not necessarily a physical death like Bonhoeffer's, who was hung by the Nazis for his participation in the plot to assassinate Hitler, but always a death of self in separation from other selves. Following the Jesus Way means that we can't live like the vast majority of human beings live, and this can cause us a great deal of trouble.

But the good news in all this is that God, rather than our limited knowledge and understanding, is the source of our calling and the source of our strength. What makes it "good news" is that, in those moments when we understandably have had enough of this life and cannot trust God, God has not had enough of us. So, rather than turning to our knowledge, perhaps we can turn to the historical Jesus as the Christ of faith, recognizing that we certainly cannot have enough of him. And when put that way, it is a wonder that we aren't so drawn to the Bread of Life that we double back into the line at communion in order to get seconds.

So here it is. The Pharisees of the historical Jesus' time, just like the Pharisees of our time, thought of the Kingdom of God as a future reality, a not-yet state of perfected existence other than what we experience here-and-now, a perfected existence we have to earn by our deeds in the here-and-now. Jesus didn't think this was the case at all. For him, the Kingdom of God—or a better translation, the "the Commonwealth of God"—was both a future and present here-and-now reality. We experience the Commonwealth of God here-and-now whenever the hungry are fed, wherever the sick have access to adequate health care, wherever justice is upheld, wherever systemic forms of social, political, racial, gender, and environmental oppression are resisted. For God is on the side of the marginalized and the oppressed. In other words, we experience the Commonwealth of God here-and-now in whatever place and time we occupy, where all of us, right now, are sitting at the place of honor that is everyplace because we are so interdependent that the suffering of one of us is the suffering of all of us, just as the joy of one of us is the joy of all of us. We don't have to wait for the future because the future is already here. We don't have to wait for a future Messianic banquet, because we participate in this banquet every time we share the Eucharist. And there is no place of honor, other than the particular place we occupy at the moment we show up, with utter disregard for all those conventional labels we use to define ourselves in separation from everyone else—an expression of God's grace that floods over the universe like a waterfall—or a tidal wave.

4

When Law and Compassion Conflict

> Deuteronomy 5:12–21
> Psalm 139:1–6, 13–18
> 2 Corinthians 4:5–2
> Mark 2:23—3:6

It's a sad fact that more often than not, obedience to legal systems and the practice of compassion often collide head on. According to the prophet Micah, who lived in rather turbulent times in the eighth century BCE as the Assyrian empire was in the process of invading Israel, God requires human beings to "do justice, practice compassion," and on this foundation, "create solidarity of community" (Micah 6:8; trans. mine). All of the Hebraic prophets agreed that this was the whole purpose of the Torah revealed to Moses on Mount Sinai. But what does justice mean and how does it interrelate with compassion, and how can justice and compassion be the center of a legal system.

The Word *torah* means "Instruction" and refers to the principles upon which human beings should create *halakah* or "laws" reflecting the Torah's "instruction" that human beings live justly, compassionately, and on this foundation, create solidarity of community. But what happens when laws are so hardened by legal systems that justice, compassion, and solidarity of community simply disappear? This is an issued raised by not only the Gospel of Mark, but all the gospels and Pauline epistles. The two controversy scenes in Mark 2:23—3:6, one in a grain field and one in a synagogue, illuminate why the leaders of the Jerusalem temple, the "priests" or "Sadducees" and some leaders of synagogues known as rabbis, found Jesus so offensive and saw him as a grave danger.

And the rub is that Jesus' controversies with the temple leaders are also difficult for many contemporary Christians to understand, given that so many Christians default to defective notions of first-century Judaism and unhelpful caricatures of Jesus's outlook on the relationship between Torah and *halakah*. The story begins with Jesus' disciples literally making their way through grain fields. They are not *stealing* grain. What concerns the Pharisees instead is the fact that they are traveling and gleaning on the sabbath. They should have stayed put and prepared their snacks on the previous day. To the Pharisees, this behavior appears to deliberately neglect the mandate to observe the sabbath and keep it holy. But Jesus disagreed, not because he regarded the sabbath commandments as trivial, but because he saw a larger picture, one that regards the sabbath in a different light.

So, he turned to another piece of tradition, a story about David to interpret the purpose of the sabbath, found in what is now referred to as 1 Samuel 21:1–6—a story about David taking consecrated bread that was supposed to be reserved for the temple's priests. David took the bread because he was a fugitive, seeking allies as he fled from Saul, who had clearly declared his intentions to kill him. Jesus implies that the priest, whom the author of Mark misidentifies as Abiathar instead of Ahimelech, did nothing wrong in breaking the strict letter of the *halakah* concerning the bread. By remedying David's hunger, the priest sustained the life of a weary traveler and contributed to David's quest to live into his calling as the king anointed to replace Saul.

In other words, Jesus—like any good rabbi—offers a legal opinion, one derived from precedent derived from the Torah itself. He argues that sometimes certain demands of *halakah* are rightly set aside in favor of pursuing greater values or meeting greater needs, especially when those greater needs promote a person's well-being and facilitate the arrival of divine blessings. But Jesus's argument is hardly novel and therefore not particularly scandalous. In fact, when he notes that the purpose of the sabbath has always been to serve humankind, as opposed to making humankind serve some stern legalistic religious principle, he is essentially restating Deuteronomy 5:12–15, in which God institutes the sabbath so a people who once toiled in slavery can forever enjoy at least a modicum of rest. Rabbinic traditions dating to a century after Jesus' death expressed opinions similar to his words in Mark 2:27, including: "The Sabbath is handed over to you, not you to it"; and "Profane one Sabbath for a person's sake, so that he may keep many Sabbaths." The proper function of the sabbath is to promote life and extol God as a liberator.

The Pharisees certainly understood the sabbath. Perhaps they did not appreciate that it was Jesus, by some appearances a new teacher, dispensing legal insights. Where Jesus definitely would have caught their attention was in his assumption that somehow, he and his calling were comparable to David and David's calling. Also, declaring himself the "lord" or "master" of the sabbath itself could be tantamount to claiming that *halakah*'s ultimate purpose is to serve Jesus. The scandal resides here: he presented himself as no ordinary teacher.

The scene in the synagogue intensifies the conflict over Jesus' authority, his values, and the urgency of his claims. For the Pharisees the issue was not whether Jesus had the power to heal a man's hand, but whether doing so on the sabbath demonstrated a willful disregard for the Torah that was believed to give good order to life and to provide conditions for encountering God's blessings and holiness. Jesus' response to the Pharisees—"Is it lawful to do good or to do harm on the sabbath, to save life or to kill?"—indicates that he disagrees with the premise of their question. By healing the man's hand, Jesus did not disparage or break the Torah's demand to keep the sabbath because nothing Jesus did in this intance can be considered "work" that the sabbath forbids. In other words, Mark casts Jesus as honoring the purposes underlying the sabbath commandment. It is as if Jesus is saying that the chief objective of Torah and *halakah* is to save and preserve life. Indeed, what better day is there than the sabbath, a day meant to promote God's commitment to humanity's well-being, for the restoration of a man's malformed hand? Furthermore, Jesus' contemporaries would not have found his basic perspective particularly troublesome. "Saving life overrules the Sabbath," according to ancient rabbinic tradition.

Admittedly, this unnamed man was not dying, but his hand was withered. Jesus's act of healing demonstrated the urgency of his life-giving work; after all, Jesus and his followers believed the Commonwealth of God was near and many people were hoping for liberation from systemic forms of injustice. With the restoration of his hand, the man in the synagogue probably also received back his ability to work in the Galilean economy. In receiving that ability, the man could recover his ability to provide for a family. In other words, we need to avoid seeing this healing as an act of merely "fixing" something that had gone "wrong" with the man. The event represents a restoration to wholeness and dignity. Its meaning is the promotion of life and human flourishing. Foretastes of resurrection cannot wait. They extend the sabbath's joy and freedom to all aspects of life.

But the restoration of this man's hand marked the beginning of the end for the historical Jesus, according to the author of Mark. Only 79 verses into this Gospel, and now the Pharisees and Herodians want to destroy him. Even though those two groups are not mentioned at all in connection with Jesus's arrest, prosecution, and execution at the end of Mark, still their partnership here, so early in the narrative, is very curious. The name "Herodians" is ambiguous. No one knows exactly to whom Mark refers with that term. But the association with Herod—and the ardent Hellenizing legacy of the Herodian family—makes them unlikely political allies for the Pharisees, who tended to resist Hellenistic influences. Yet after a very short time, Jesus has managed to offend two very different groups. Imagine the editorial staffs of both *Mother Jones* and *The National Review* finding something or someone they both vehemently oppose. In this pair of scenes, Jesus does not assail the Israelite and Judaite Ways. He does not reject Torah or *halakah*. He does not render the sabbath obsolete. He does not even call the Pharisees blind guides or a pack of dotards. Neither should an essay on this passage draw similar conclusions. But an essay on these two scenes should note the way in which disagreement about living within the boundaries of *halakah* quickly escalates into hostility, a hostility that will eventually lead some of the most powerful religious authorities to seek Jesus' debasement and death. Even as the passage emphasizes a commitment to life and vitality abiding at the heart of God's reign, it also illustrates how religious commitments and values, *any* religious teaching and practice, can turn oppressive in the hands of legalistic religious leaders.

Thus, the entire Gospel of Mark tells a story of recurring controversy. Passages like this help us interpret the controversies between Jesus and the religious leaders of his day because for the author of Mark, the cross is a sober reminder of how easily the most noble motives can be perverted. It points out how quickly an institution can become a law unto itself, stifling the legitimate concerns of those outside that may seem to threaten stability. It illustrates how frequently insidious forces we scarcely notice can transform the best-educated, best-intentioned among us into insensitive leaders, desperately out of touch with what's real.

Such insensitivity and brokenness move Jesus to grief in the synagogue when he considers the stony, Pharaoh-like hearts that regard institutions as more valuable than removing suffering and disadvantage before the sun sets. But Mark also has good news to announce. This story of the in-breaking reign of God will also tell of compassion and transformation. Jesus, like the God who instituted the sabbath, is committed to preserving life. His life and death expose the oppressive and corrosive tyrannies of fear, imperial pretense, and religious hypocrisy, wherever they reside.

— 5 —

The Bloody Truth

> 1 Kings 8:1–11, 22–30
> Psalm 84
> Ephesians 6:10–20
> John 6:56–69

When Jesus told people that his flesh was food and his blood was drink, and on top of this, eating his flesh and drinking his blood would lead to eternal life, many people cut and ran. Even the disciples grumbled among themselves about how hard a teaching this was. Jesus had to ask the disciples if they wanted to walk away too. So, what was the problem? The answer, and the point Jesus was trying to make, lies deep in the seventeenth chapter of Leviticus, which contains a forceful and simple law or *halakah* about how the people of God were to handle their food. In Leviticus 17:10–14, we read:

> If anyone of the house of Israel or of the aliens who reside among them eats any blood, I will set my face against that person who eats blood, and will cut that person off from the people. For the life of the flesh is in the blood; and I have given it to you for making atonement for your lives on the altar; for, as life, it is the blood that makes atonement. Therefore I have said to the people of Israel: No person among you shall eat blood, nor shall any alien who resides among you eat blood. And anyone of the people of Israel, or of the aliens who reside among them, who hunts down an animal or bird that may be eaten

shall pour out its blood and cover it with earth. For the life of every creature—its blood is its life; therefore I have said to the people of Israel: You shall not eat the blood of any creature, for the life of every creature is its blood; whoever eats it shall be cut off.

There seems to be no wiggle room in this passage. Those who follow God's "Instructions" or Torah must never consume blood. End of discussion. There are no circumstances where this law can be broken or swept aside. Ignoring this law means that you are cut off from God—forever. This and other dietary laws were deeply ingrained in the daily life of all who followed God's Torah. It a basic law ingrained in Israelite and Judean religious practices; and it's still a cornerstone of much contemporary Jewish eating habits. Any slaughterhouse in the United States that produces meat that bears the identification "kosher" follows Leviticus 17:10–14.

So, when the writer of the Gospel of John portrays Jesus instructing a crowd of people that in order to inherit eternal life they must eat his body and drink his blood, the writer was using incendiary language that contradicted a millennium of teaching and practice that seems to place Jesus' teaching credentials into serious question. It would have a made his disciples question whether they could still follow him. All of Jesus's followers must have experienced a double-take as they uttered under their breath, "Huh?"

However today for most Christians, Jesus' instruction about eating his body and drinking his blood do not raise much consternation. In particular, Christians from more "sacramental" communities and liturgical traditions—Roman Catholic, Greek Orthodox, Lutheran, Methodist, Presbyterian, Anglican—hear in Jesus's words a direct reference to the Eucharist. For Christians who participate in the breaking of bread and sharing wine each and every Sunday, this teaching from the sixth chapter of John is an obvious allusion to a sacrament they know so well. And yet, I seriously doubt that what the writer of John was thinking about contemporary liturgical practice.

Still, most biblical scholars and theologians identify the Gospel of John as the "most Eucharistic" of the four gospels. Between the Bread of Life discourses and the feeding of the multitudes, there's enough evidence to support this conclusion. And yet there is no story of the Last Supper in John. According to John, on the night before Jesus' death he gets up from the table to wash his disciples' feet. But John doesn't say anything about a "last supper." The source of disgust in Jesus's listeners is God's clear prohibition of consuming blood in Leviticus 17. And I think that Leviticus 17 is exactly what John's portrayal of Jesus was getting at, but by a different route. Leviticus 17:14 says: "For the life of every creature—its blood is its life; therefore I have said to the people of Israel: You shall not eat the blood of any creature, for the life of every creature is its blood; whoever eats it shall be cut off."

Blood wasn't forbidden because it was dirty, but because blood, along with breath, is a life force and therefore sacred. Accordingly, a good portion of Leviticus is concerned with what to do with the blood and body parts of sacrificial animals. When animals were sacrificed to God in the rituals that are carefully laid out in Leviticus, various portions of the carcass were given back to the person making the offering and to the priests to consume or burn on the altar. But the animal's blood was always given to God. Usually it was poured onto the altar directly. Why? Because the blood of the animal is the life of an animal. In other words, along with breath, the life force that enlivens all living beings is its blood. Because God is the giver of all life, life is sacred; and life is not to be misused or mistreated—and certainly not consumed. Life belongs to God, and God alone.

So, when Jesus says that his followers are to drink his blood, what he's saying in the ancient biblical language of Leviticus is: "take my life and pour it into your lives." And by pouring his eternal life-blood into our lives, John thinks we are the recipients of eternal life ourselves, because the historical Jesus as the Christ of faith's life is coursing in our lives.

— 6 —

Jesus and James on "True Religion"

> Song of Solomon 2:8–13
> Psalm 15
> James 1:17–17
> Mark 7:1–8, 14–15, 23

I have a Jewish friend who tries hard to "keep *kosher*" by eating only what is "fit" or "clean"—from the Hebrew word *kasher*. Following purity laws or *halakah* is an important discipline for our Jewish sisters and brothers—particularly Conservative and Orthodox Jews—as a means of cementing their relationship with God. I've always admired the discipline required for following *halakah* because as the most persecuted religious community in the history of the world's Religious Ways, Jews remained visibly loyal to God by following the distinctive *halakah* that defined the meaning of loyalty to God as embodied in God's Torah, while simultaneously bring an example of what loyalty to God required of non-Jewish communities. As Deutero-Isaiah put it twenty-five hundred years ago, following the distinctive requirements of *halakah*—from refraining from eating certain kinds of food to the distinctive forms of Jewish dress, prayer, and ethical behavior—publicly demonstrates that the Jewish people are "a light to the nations" (Isaiah 49:6).

Throughout the Gospel of Mark, ritual purity is the context for the mission and message of the historical Jesus. Dietary restrictions were only a small part of a comprehensive "holiness code" that regulated every aspect of personal and communal life for the followers of Torah in Israel and Judah. By one count, there are 631 *mizvot* or "commandments" in the five books of Moses. The purity laws of Leviticus 11–26, for example, describe clean and unclean foods, purity rituals after childbirth or a menstrual cycle, regulations for skin infections and contaminated clothing or furniture, prohibitions against contact with a human corpse or dead animal, instructions about nocturnal emissions, laws regarding bodily discharges, agricultural guidelines about planting seeds and mating animals, decrees about lawful sexual relationships, keeping the sabbath, forsaking idols, and even tattoos.

Why so many rules? Some of these purity laws encoded common sense or moral ideals that we still follow today, like prohibitions against incest. Others regulated hygiene and sanitation. Still others symbolized Israel's unique identity that differentiated its people from pagan nations. At their best, the purity laws ritualized an exhortation from Yahweh: "Be holy because I, the LORD your God, am holy." When Psalm 15 asks, "LORD, who may dwell in your sanctuary?" the right response is that only people who are "pure" may approach God.

We don't know much about how ordinary first-century Judeans maintained ritual purity, but the Pharisees about whom we read so much in the gospels certainly are portrayed as doing so. Throughout the gospels they criticized Jesus for his flagrant disregard for ritual purity: Jesus the Jew touched a leper (Mark 1:41); his disciples didn't fast (Mark 2:18–19); Jesus and his disciples ignored sabbath laws (2:23–24); he touched a menstruating woman and handled a corpse (5:21–42); and healed two Gentiles (Mark 7:24–25).

In Mark 7:3–5, the writer recounts a clash between Jesus and the Pharisees about food purity. The Pharisees complained that Jesus's disciples ate with "unclean" hands. Verse 5 includes two parenthetical explanations to his Gentile readers, who otherwise might have been clueless: the Pharisees and all the Judeans do not eat unless they thoroughly wash their hands, thus observing the tradition of the elders; and they do not eat anything from the market unless they wash it; and there are also many other traditions they observe like the washing of cups, pots, and bronze kettles. Then, in an aside that we might find trivial, but his Judean readers would have found shocking, Mark writes that Jesus declared all foods "clean" (verses 9–14). Say what?

The thing to notice is the central accusation in this clash between the Pharisees and Jesus. The Pharisees thought Jesus and his followers were ritually unclean sinners who flaunted God's *halakah*. They were "dirty" and "impure." And in a sense, they were right. Given our propensity to justify ourselves and to scapegoat others, the purity laws lent themselves to a spiritual stratification or hierarchy between the ritually "clean," who considered themselves to be close to God, and the "unclean," who were shunned as impure sinners and far from God. So instead of expressing the holiness of God, ritual purity became a means of excluding people considered dirty, polluted, or contaminated. In word and action Jesus ignored, disregarded, and actively demolished all distinctions of ritual purity as a measure of spiritual status.

My favorite New Testament scholar, Marcus Borg, argued that Jesus turned the purity system with its "sharp social boundaries" on its head. In its place he substituted a radically alternate social vision.[1] The new community that Jesus announced would be characterized by compassion for everyone in place of external compliance to a purity code, by egalitarian inclusivity rather than hierarchical exclusivity, and by inward transformation rather than outward ritual performance. In place of "be holy, for I am holy" (Leviticus 19:2), Jesus deliberately substituted the call to "be merciful, just as your Father is merciful" (Luke 6:36). No outcasts were cast out far enough in Jesus's world to make him shun them—not Roman collaborators, not lepers, not prostitutes, not the crazed, not the possessed. No one could possibly be outside God's encompassing love.

Just as Jesus warned of "worshiping in vain," the Epistle of James draws a distinction between religious practices that are either "worthless" or "faultless," either "true" or "defiled." The difference between the two has to do with self-deception. "Don't be deceived,"

---

1. Borg, *Meeting Jesus Again for the First Time*, 49–57.

he writes. All the good gifts in anyone's life "come from the Father above" (James 1:17). In a striking description, James says that "God gives generously to all without finding fault." The fiction of the self-made person is just that, a fiction. It's a self-deception. "Don't deceive yourselves," James repeats. "Don't merely listen to the gospel, and so deceive yourselves. Do what it says." To listen without doing is like looking at your face in a mirror, walking away, and then forgetting what you look like. And then a third time: "If any think they are religious, and do not bridle their tongues but deceive their hearts, their religion is worthless" (1:22–26). James compares the power of speech to a bit in a horse's mouth, a small rudder that steers a large ship, or a tiny spark that ignites a huge forest fire (3:1-6). So as Jesus contrasted outward obedience with inward compassion, James contrasts "worthless" religion that is self-deceptive with the "faultless" religion of caring for widows and orphans (1:27).

When I was a student at the Claremont School of Theology, I came across a prayer by Søren Kierkegaard that warns against "self-deception" (James) and confusing "rules" with the Commands of God (Jesus) that I wrote down on a piece of paper and carried around until I lost it:

> Lord! Give us weak eyes
> for things that do not matter
> and eyes full of clarity
> in all your truth.

— 7 —

A Woman of Faith

Psalm 124
James 2;1–17
Mark 7:24–37

I have to admit that the story of Jesus's encounter with the Syrophonenician woman in Mark 7:24–37 has caused me a lot of necessary grief. "Necessary" because of the way in which my feminist theologian friends have opened my eyes to the nastiness of the patriarchal oppression of women in all religious and secular institutions and social systems throughout human history, an oppression that assumes that men are superior to women and need men's supervision, even when it comes to reproduction. Men are supposedly "in charge" because women are weak, guided by emotional responses, irrational, and incapable of equal status with men. The historical Jesus was raised within a patriarchal social order created by a patriarchal religious system.

As a university professor for forty-four years, I have lost count of the number women I have met who are like the woman Jesus met. I know her because I have seen the desperate, pleading looks in their eyes, heard the grief-stricken yearning in their voices. My guess is that most people reading this reflection have encountered someone like her too—a women who will travel any distance, cross over any barriers, risk any social shame to save the life of her child, sibling, parent, or friend. We know her well and recognize her deep struggle, so that is it any wonder that we should be troubled by Jesus's initial response to her? In fact, every commentary on Mark 7:24–37 I have read seems unable to adequately explain or "explain away" Jesus's dehumanization of this woman by comparing her suffering child to a dog.

Perhaps one might surmise that Jesus was just tired. That perhaps his retreat into the region of Tyre was meant to be just that: a retreat from the constant pressure bearing down on him from countless needy, suffering people and those in authority who tried stand in the way of what he felt called to do. Maybe Jesus's weariness is what is heard in his seemingly instinctive response. Perhaps this is the case. After all, the historical Jesus was human, a man raised in the patriarchal traditions of his day who at times treated women very harshly. And even though his inner circle included a large number of women, there is no piece of scripture that more clearly reveals his culture's attitude towards women than this.

But as a process theologian, I cannot help but wonder if this story is a powerful reminder that the historical Jesus and the God he experienced are not unchanging. The historical Jesus was certainly shaped and influenced by his culture and history, born into and living in a particular time and place with all that meant. Indeed, as a human being, Jesus was a "work in process" as he was transformed into the one who would lay down his life not just for those who came from the same place that he did, but for all the rest of us as well. There is certainly evidence in the Bible that God's interaction with the world changes God: Abraham's argument with God that Sodom be should spared from God's destructive anger (Genesis 18:16–33); or the story about Jesus eating his last meal with the twelve disciples, or the image of Mary in John's Gospel kneeling to anoint his feet, which he repeated by kneeling before his disciples as he washed their feet a few days later (John 12;1–8, John 13:1–11). Perhaps the historical Jesus was changed by what his female disciples did for him.

In the end, I must confess that I am not now, nor ever will be, comfortable with the portrayal of Jesus in the story of his encounter with Syrophonenician woman. I also know this because:

- Jesus stepped into actual situations with women where he would not be "at home." In doing so he was automatically more accessible to those with whom he would perhaps share little other than a common humanity.
- Though his words may have been meant to dismiss her and her ill child, he did not ignore them.
- And Jesus was not above admitting that he was outwitted in the theological exchange they shared. Though not explicitly said, by granting her heart's desire for her suffering daughter, he admits he has been bested.
- Indeed, because Jesus was open to having his mind changed, he was open to being changed. He was willing to be moved.

So might it be that if Jesus could be changed—if Jesus' imagination could be expanded to understand that God's love and grace and healing and power were meant for all people—might our love, grace, and struggle for justice be stretched as well? I am suggesting that the fact that the historical Jesus underwent processes of change and becoming indicates that our relationship with the historical Jesus Christians confess to be the Christ of faith is meant to be just as lively.

Accordingly, the short story of Jesus's encounter with the Syrophonenician woman challenges patriarchal assumptions in several interdependent ways: the Syrophonenician woman gets her daughter healed; she is a woman who disdains social status more than men do; she is an insightful woman who possesses more wisdom than the disciples and the historical Jesus; she is a religiously "impure" person who has greater access to God than the "pure" male leaders of Israel; and accordingly, her story leads hearers (and in our case, readers) to overcome conventional hostilities that set artificial limits to membership in the Commonwealth of God.

All of this became clear to me as I read the story of the Syrophonenician woman contextualized by the Epistle of James 2:1–17, particularly verse 17: "So faith, by itself, if it has no works, is dead." As a Lutheran, I do not find this assertion contrary to Paul's, Augustine's, or Luther's emphasis that, in Luther's language, human beings are "justified by grace through faith alone." Turning "faith and works" into a reductionistic doctrinal dualism misses at best, and destroys at worst, the meaning of "faith" and "works," particularly as these two interdependent polarities come together in the story of Jesus's encounter with the Syrophonenician woman. She called out Jesus to do more than talk because in the act of begging for food for her ill child, she demonstrated that "faith, by itself, if it has no works, is dead." In fact, faith without works isn't faith at all.

Furthermore, in this story, "faith" did not mean, nor has it ever meant—except in the theologies of most Fundamentalist and many forms of Evangelical theology—"belief." We do not *believe* ourselves *into* a state of faith, we *find* ourselves in a state of faith, and act and believe accordingly, which is the meaning of "works." Faith means "trust," betting one's life on," "being committed to," "being guided by" a Sacred Reality named differently in the world's religious Ways, but which is named "God" in the Jewish, Christian, and Islamic Ways. But once we experience being in a state of faith, we have to interpret the meaning of the experience, which entails theological reflection, doctrines, or "beliefs." "Beliefs" are opinions we hold about the meaning of our experience of being in a state of faith. As such, "beliefs" can be elegant, rational, irrational, stupid, false or true, doctrinal propaganda, or pointers toward the Sacred reality Christians name God. But God cannot be reduced to a set of doctrinal propositions or "beliefs.

In other words, Syrophonenician woman was the historical Jesus's theological instructor whose example creatively transformed him—because he listened and responded appropriately—on his way to becoming the Christ of faith.

— 8 —

Who Did the Historical Jesus Say He Was?

Proverbs 1:20–23
Psalm 19
James 3:1–12
Mark 8:27–38

I wear two methodological hats, that of a historian of religions and that of a Lutheran process theologian. A historian of religions treats religious experience, doctrines, and practices as descriptive "objective facts" to be reported, placed in historical contexts, compared, and analyzed without asserting whether or not this "data" corresponds to anything that reflects reality, meaning "the way things really are." "Normative questions" of beauty, good and evil, and truth, or how should human beings live with each other and with the life forms with whom we share this planet are simply left out in this form of religious studies because they are "subjective." The theory of knowledge or "epistemology" underlying history of religions, indeed most Western academic disciplines, goes back to the seventeenth-century founder of the Enlightenment, René Descartes, who summarized his mind-body dualism in a slogan-like statement: *cogito ergo sum*, or "I think therefore I am."

But theological reflection focuses on "normative questions": questions of value, truth, beauty, goodness, the meaning of life in the face of the objective reality of death. I have always been suspicious of reducing history of religions to a set of methodologies for

WHO DID THE HISTORICAL JESUS SAY HE WAS?

describing religious "matters of fact" and theology to normative issues of truth raised by these "facts." So about twelve years ago, my theology professor, John Cobb, and I were sitting in his apartment in Claremont, California, getting "caught up" on my latest writing project, when what seemed out of nowhere, he said, "You know Paul, you're a theologian."

"I thought I was a historian of religions," I replied with some surprise.

"You are, but theology is about seeking the truth no matter where it leads you and no matter what cultural or religious dress it wears. Academic disciplines need to be integrated."

Gradually as I thought about our conversation, it became clear that what he said to me was, in Luther's words in his *Small Catechism*, "most certainly true." Accordingly, I now wear two methodological hats simultaneously—that of a historian of religions and that of a process theologian, without apology to my colleagues in history of religions or my colleagues in theology. The most important questions we face center on the meanings and values of matters of fact.

This is certainly illustrated by Jesus's question to his disciples recorded in Mark 8:27-38: "Who do you say that I am?"—a question that cannot be answered as a mere description of the historical Jesus—his place of birth, his occupation as a carpenter, his physical appearance, his gender, his religious identity, his work as a teacher in a world of teachers and healers. These "facts" and "labels" do not define who Jesus was any more than the facts and labels of our lives define who we are. But here's the hiccup: these facts and labels were part of who the historical Jesus was to the people who knew him and to whom he asked the question, "Who do you say that I am?"

Here's another hiccup. It is interesting to the point of amazement that the author of James, who wrote this epistle in the late first or early second century, seems so interdependent with Mark's account of the historical Jesus written in 70 C.E. Tradition identifies the author of James as the brother of Jesus, who was the leader of the Jerusalem church until his martyrdom prior to the

Judean–Roman War of 66–70 C.E. James the brother of Jesus was certainly not the author of the Epistle of James, yet James 3:1–12 provides an important clarification of the meaning of Jesus's question to his disciples by using some rather evocative imagery to make two important points, each embedded in the other and each reinforcing a critical message: what we say matters.

James likens both points to the bit in a horses' mouth and the rudder to the tongue, which was his way directing our attention to the words we use, the things we say. The tongue is to the body as the bit is to the horse and the rudder to the ship, which is say that each image is about providing direction: the rider uses a bit to direct the path taken by a horse and the speed at which it goes; the rudder sets the course for the ship. Likewise, the tongue or our speech reflects our character and the direction our lives have taken or will take. "Choose your words well," James advises.

Good conventional advice: speech directs action; action reflects character. The one is indicative of, or reveals, the other. At this point the writer of James seems to be making the "as without, so within" argument—as the tongue guides one's character, so the bridle guides the horse. But then he takes his argument upstream, so to speak, and adds the image of a spring, which pours forth water (3:11). The same source cannot produce both fresh, clean water and brackish water—no more than a fig tree can grow grapes. So now James appears to be making the opposite point: "as within, so without." At the source, it must be one or the other; it cannot be both. So what the hell was the writer of James getting at?

At this point, it's useful to contextualize all this with a powerful theme of previous chapters, where the writer of James declares the hypocrisy of "faith" that is merely spoken, or professed, without the actions that inevitably manifest from authentic faith. In other words, faith without works is dead and religion without compassion is worthless, just as the hypocrite who says one thing and does another is actively practicing deceit. It may be self-deception, or it may be deliberate lies, but the water at the source is brackish. No matter how eloquently crafted, speech that springs from brackish water cannot be clean.

WHO DID THE HISTORICAL JESUS SAY HE WAS?

"Watch what we do, not what we say" was a line famously uttered by Attorney General John Mitchell at the start of the Nixon administration. It was intended to reassure African Americans that despite what the Nixon administration was *saying* to pacify white Southerners, what they would actually *do* is move toward desegregation. When we hear this phrase today, we are more likely to take it the other way: spouting fine words about patriotism or religion while acting in reprehensible ways; using words to distract, to disguise, to disparage, to deceive. Reporters used to call it "spin" and accuse politicians of it; now politicians call it "fake news" and accuse news reporters of it. Words intended to manipulate truth, to present "alternate facts," to incite violence—whether uttered in speeches, issued in tweets, or turned into chants—are words that spring from a brackish source. Public speech that is crafted to deceive is manipulative, and it has two targets: truth and trust. If we can be persuaded to doubt what is true, then we will no longer know whom we can trust. Distrust leads to isolation, and isolation makes us easy prey for despots.

But speech that uplifts, that encourages, that teaches wisdom, that resonates as true is speech that springs from a pure heart. And that is what James is ultimately aiming for. His fuming against hypocrisy is a plea for its opposite: integrity. And it's at this point that the writer of James adds clarification to Jesus's question to his disciples in Mark 8:27–38.

Much has been made of the "messianic secret" in Mark—the term scholars have variously used, rejected, or revived to explain why Jesus enjoins his followers, those he heals, and the demons he casts out, to tell no one that he is the Messiah. While the "messianic secret" has always mystified me, the most important point in Mark's gospel is not the "messianic secret," but what Jesus appears to be teaching about messianic expectations. Everything in Mark revolves around Jesus's question to his disciples; from chapter eight until the conclusion of Mark, there is a shift in narrative sites from seas, boats and wilderness to a journey from the margins of Palestine to the extreme north of Caesarea Philippi southward to Jerusalem. Jesus and the disciples are "on the Way," when Jesus asks them—and us who read Mark—"Who do you say that I am?" Peter answers, "You are the Messiah." Jesus then instructs them not to tell anyone about him, but he also begins to teach them openly about the suffering and death that await him. For this, Peter rebukes him, but then Jesus surprises Peter—and us—with his vehement response, saying to Peter, "Get behind me, Satan!"

So what gives? Why does Peter rebuke Jesus, and why does Jesus, in his reply, bring up his temptation in the desert (Mark 1:13)? The key to unlocking this odd exchange is in the verses that follow, which essentially explain Jesus' theology of reversal and what he understands to be the meaning of "messiah." If the outcome of following the Jesus Way is suffering, rejection, and death, then his model of discipleship was clearly not based on imperial Rome, with its military might, its royal aggrandizement, and its ostentatious wealth. Instead, Jesus taught a reversal of how the world understands power, and Peter, by failing to understand Jesus's meaning, appears in the guise of Satan, trying once again to tempt Jesus with Caesar's kind of power. So, transported two thousand years into our world, the character of contemporary Christian faith hangs on how we answer the question, "Who do you say that I am?"

Jesus used numerous parables to instruct the disciples about the kingdom of God that bears no resemblance to Roman domination of the world. The kingdom of God, or better "The Commonwealth of God," is the opposite of the empire of Caesar, so it stands to reason that Jesus would not use the Roman tools of conquest and domination to establish God's Commonwealth on earth. The reversal of one—the true meaning of power—calls for reversal of the other—the true meaning of discipleship.

The ideal of reversal is a central notion in process theology. God's power is persuasive, not coercive or domineering. There is a metaphysical explanation for this that has to do with genuine free will and the integral creative presence of God in the natural world. But this is not something that process folks figured out and then imposed on the Christian Way. When Alfred North Whitehead was grappling with the creative dynamism of the universe, he found an interpretive key in what he called "the Galilean origin of Christianity" that "slowly and in quietness operate(s) by love." Unfortunately, as Whitehead also observed, this "brief Galilean vision of humility" has only "flickered" down through the ages. Indeed, the Christian Way, from the moment the Roman Emperor Constantine made it the official religion of his empire, has been characterized by Caesar. Or as Whitehead writes, "When the Western world accepted Christianity, Caesar conquered."

This is why James's epistle and the question posed by Jesus— "Who do you say that I am?"—is one that must be asked of every generation, in every historical era. And to simply answer, "You are the Messiah," is not enough. The more crucial question is the follow-up: how do we understand that word, "messiah"? Has Caesar conquered, or can we reclaim that "Galilean vision of humility"? Do we want our notions of leadership and power shaped by the likes of Der Führer and Il Duce—or Donald Trump? Or by someone else claiming to be the greatest, a super genius, who has the best words? Or do we want these notions to be shaped by a power that operates slowly and quietly, through love? What do *we* say? We must choose our words wisely, because what we teach, what we preach, what we say privately, or what we proclaim publicly—these days, everything we say—matters.

— 9 —

The Death of Jesus and the Future of Violence

Jeremiah 11:18–20
Psalm 1
James 3:13—4:3–8
Mark 9:30–37

If there was ever a time for the words recorded in Jeremiah, Psalm 1, and James to sink in, it is now, when nations worldwide are so divided. The problem is violent factionalism, not only in the normal conflicts that arise within communities at all times and in all places, but also those that arise in wider social-political contexts. The difficulty is the impulse to assign blame. Or in the words of the Epistle of James, which side demonstrates a "gentleness born of wisdom" (James 3:13) and which side is rife with "envy and selfish ambition" (3:16). Although the condemnatory language in James is pointedly singleminded and to the point, the unknown author of this epistle actually focuses on the question of how best to respond to the polarizing demands of difficult times. And like the rest of the Bible, James's worldview is the three-tiered universe of antiquity, so that God's wisdom is visualized as coming from "above."

Process theologians like me understand "the wisdom from above" as God's persuasive presence at every moment, always aimed at the well-being of every creature with whom we share life on this planet. God's wisdom is "first pure, then peaceful, gentle, willing to yield, full of mercy and good fruits, without a trace of partiality or hypocrisy" (3:17). But a warning from feminist process theologians is in order: because of the patriarchal assumptions that run throughout the Bible, phrases like "willing to yield" needs some interpretation. "To yield" has a sense of giving up control or responsibility because we are forced to. But if one yields in the sense that James is suggesting, then there is no loss of control or agency. One is not "forced" into something that is actually, and for strategic reasons, purposefully chosen. To yield strategically then invokes the meaning of the noun form: yield as the production of something positive or beneficial.

This divine wisdom is contrasted with the wisdom of the world, which is envious, ambitious, "unspiritual, devilish" (3:15), leading to "disorder and wickedness of every kind" (3:16). In other words, there are two ways of understanding wisdom, just as there are two ways of understanding power (God's and Caesar's), or two ways of understanding religion (authentic, based on compassion; and "worthless," based on hypocrisy). There are also two ways of resistance. In process-relational terms, in every moment of our lives we are confronted with our past, our present situation, and a novel suggestion or "aim" from God. All of these offer us a possible way forward. We can repeat the past, succumb to our era's dominant ethos, or act on a creative suggestion from God. To trust that God is always present is to open ourselves to that presence and invite God's wisdom. Or as James puts it in 4:7: "Draw near to God, and God will draw hear to you."

So according to James's worldview, there is the choice between "earthly" wisdom and wisdom from "above." Each kind of "wisdom" produces its own consequences. Each kind also produces its own list of descriptive adjectives, but James lays his heaviest emphasis on peace and peacemaking. This is offset by words like "war," "murder," "disputes," and "conflicts" (3:17, 18; 4:1, 2). In verse 3:14, "bitter envy and selfish ambition" are best translated as "harsh zeal" and "fanatical devotion to a cause," which suggests a conflict bitter enough to provoke violence, or at the least to raise violence as a possible form of resistance.

The Greek word often translated as "rivalry" or "strife" is better understood as "the service of a party, party spirit, or faction." The "disorder" that results is a political term used since Alexander the Great's time to describe "a self-seeking pursuit of political office by unfair means," leading to instability, even insurrection and anarchy. Accordingly, one possible interpretation of the historical context of James's epistle is that his Christian community is under threat, and in response the people have split into two factions: those advocating for nonviolent resistance and those advocating for violent, destabilizing action.

In many contemporary circumstances world-wide democracy is in crisis. What is the appropriate form of resistance? James actually has two pieces of advice for us: the obvious appeal is to nonviolence, but also something more subtle, discernible in the phrase "without a trace of partiality." By that I take it that James means for us to respect one another. If I treat both friend and foe impartially, then I make no judgmental distinctions between them. I don't have to like or agree with someone to treat them with respect. If there is an overarching theme in James, it is not the things we usually think of—his railing against hypocrisy or the verse about faith without works that so irritated Martin Luther. The overarching theme would be his plea for us not to be "double-minded" (4:8); literally, of two minds, one following the wisdom of the world and the other following the wisdom of God. Live with "purity of heart," which is to say, live with integrity. Manifest God's wisdom: seek peace; respect others. This is the heart of the Epistle of James and also an entry point into Mark 9:30–37.

In this text, Jesus again instructs his disciples about his "theology of reversal" because they clearly haven't understood what he was getting at. As they arrive in Capernaum, Jesus asked, "What were you arguing about on the way?" (literally, on the path of discipleship). They were talking about which one of them was the greatest. In other words, they were "on the way," but headed in the wrong direction. So, Jesus again teaches reversal, saying, "Whoever wants to be first must be last of all and servant of all" (9:36). Then he offers a child as an example. "Whoever welcomes one such child," be begins, and in so doing signifies the importance not just of the child but of the relationship of the disciples to the child. That is, whatever he may be implying about the value of the child, his teaching is relational—in this case, about social relationships, and thus the structure of society.

"The Way" Jesus was talking about is the "Way of the cross." The Jesus Way is not just resistance to political oppression—although it is that; it also requires new forms of social organization, so that the practice of domination that has infected human relationships can be eradicated. By using a child as a teaching aid, one who was at the bottom of the social and economic scale in terms of status and rights, Jesus was basically saying, "You want to be the greatest? In the upended social world of the Commonwealth of God, here is the greatest—a child, one who in Caesar's realm is counted as the least."

This text also teaches nonviolence because it upends the violence of domination systems. Following the Jesus Way means confronting not only the politics of the world but changing our understanding of community. Which means followers of the Jesus Way must practice nonviolence in opposition to oppressive domination systems like the Roman empire or in our own time, the ideology of "making America great again." Or as Mahatma Gandhi put it, "If one does not practice nonviolence in one's personal relations with others, and hopes to use it in bigger affairs, one is vastly mistaken."

I'm not only referring to the gore and humiliation that makes the Roman practice of crucifixion so repulsive no matter who the victim is. Instead, my point has to do with considering the significance of Jesus' death. When you scratch at the surface of the claims Christians over the centuries have advanced about the cross—that in the cross, we glimpse redemptive suffering, faithful obedience even unto death, and sacrificial love—it doesn't take long to expose some real questions for Christian theological reflection. How can suffering *ever* be redemptive? What kind of divine Parent would demand such destructive obedience from a beloved Child? Why might an all-powerful and loving God need a sacrifice in order to express mercy? Is this not a theology of divine child abuse?

Such questions should spur us to reject simple explanations and make us entertain more questions, even uncomfortable ones. We must be wary of anyone who comes up with too neat and tidy a theory about exactly how Jesus' death and resurrection changes the cosmos and God's disposition toward the world. For good reason, the New Testament writings include a spectrum of metaphors, language, and claims to convey the significance of the cross. They guide our reflections on Jesus' death. But no single one of these, and no single statement, can suffice.

For example, in Mark 9:30–37, Jesus foretells his death and resurrection, one of several times he does so in Mark's account. On one level, his insights make perfect sense. Jesus certainly knew that those who, like him, assail conventional values and powerful people inevitably end up dead. On another level, the mention of his resurrection and the specificity of some of his statements about his death suggest that the predictions function to reassure the Gospels' earliest readers that the fate of God's Messiah couldn't have been an accident or a defeat. Larger forces, a deeper purpose, must have been at work in it. It was, in a way, God's own doing, according to Mark 9:31, where Jesus indicates that he "will be delivered into human hands." This statement doesn't refer exclusively to Judas, the person who will later hand him over to the authorities; rather, Jesus seems to have implied that God initiates the whole process that finally results with him executed on a Roman cross.

This is not to say that God somehow plans, engineers, or revels God's self in Jesus' being destroyed in a particular way. But it does emphasize that Jesus will become subject to human power—a power based, in this case, by self-preserving arrogance. He will do so without the protections afforded him by his prerogatives as God's emissary. Jesus will participate in the human condition without any advantage. He will experience some of humanity's most insidious displays of power, getting to know the worst of our potential up close. And so, the question lingers unanswered through time: Is God really OK with something like this? Couldn't God's relinquishment of Jesus be tantamount to moral negligence? After all, this is *God* we're talking about. Couldn't there be a neater, more peaceful solution? Again, easy answers elude us, as maybe they should.

This passage deserves a place, alongside other parts of the New Testament, in larger conversations about the crucifixion. But we cannot expect this passage on its own to answer all the questions about the purpose of Jesus' death. The same is true for questions having to do with the character and motivations of God. Instead of trying to rush to the bottom of those insoluble questions, we might first direct our focus to an audacious suggestion: that there *can* be larger purposes and beneficial outcomes to an event as horrible as a crucifixion. Could something appearing so utterly God-forsaken on the surface actually become an instrumental piece in God's active concern for humanity? Here the New Testament repeatedly insists: Yes.

Or, if we take seriously the Christian claim that God is also the one who is crucified, what happens when we consider God's willingness to suffer violence at the hands of a resistant world? God appears to be both complicit and victim at the cross, and that should catch our attention on a planet where violence is so prevalent and more often than not engaged in by people claiming to act on God's behalf. Whenever violence flares, whether religiously motivated or not, it reminds us of humankind's ferocity and our entrenched proclivities for self-preservation. It also leads us to ask whether God gives a damn about the plight of human beings. Does God like violence? Or is God finally overwhelmed by it? Or does God intend to solve the problem of human violence through divine violence? Every religious Way must grapple with these questions. They cannot be avoided if we intend to persist in hope for justice and reconciliation, things that rarely come about because people suddenly decide to lay down their weapons and try something new. By their nature, promises keep us oriented toward the future, as we repent from past wrongs and look intently for new possibilities to emerge. But promises are cheap, unless they mean something for the here and now.

And this is why Mark 9:34–37, containing Jesus' words in the aftermath of his prediction, are so important. Jesus called his followers to relinquish their own desires for power and acclaim. Instead, they must welcome those who are vulnerable and overlooked, represented by the child Jesus sets in their midst. It's a sign that Jesus' death and his return in nail-scarred resurrection might open the door to different ways of living. Is this all there is to seeing an end to violence and exploitation now? No. But it's a start.

10

A Theological Hodgepodge

Esther 7:1–6, 9–10; 9:20–22
Psalm 124
James 5:13–20
Mark: 38–50

I wonder how it is possible for any pastor to create a sermon that could possibly interrelate these four biblical texts. As texts for theological reflection it would seem that each must stand on its own exegesis or "interpretation." At least for me this seems to be the case. So what follows is my particular theological reflection on each separate text, a separation that I think cannot be unified—unless I'm missing something.

Esther 7:1-6, 9-10; 9:20-22

Like the books of Ruth and Job, the book of Esther is a work of fiction, "fiction" meaning a literary work whose content is produced by a writer's imagination in order to make important conclusions, that dates sometime in the mid-fifth century BCE. Good fiction writing may be based on historical events, like a good novel about the American Civil War that attacks the institution of slavery. But fiction is not "history," at least as history is understood today in academic circles. The historical context of Esther is set within the history of how the Persians treated the Judahite exiles after the

Cyrus the Great defeated the Babylonian empire, but the story of Esther is a work of fiction whose author is unknown.

The book of Esther is also a strange and difficult book for several reasons, first and foremost because it seems to be "non-theological." There is no mention of God. But the book of Esther is very important to our Judahite brothers and sisters because it records the deeds of a woman who was prepared to risk everything to save her people from the threat of genocide. She is the heroine and this story, which is the foundation of the Festival of Purim, at which time the whole book is read in the synagogue. Celebrated in the twelfth month of the Jewish year, it is the one Jewish holiday which centers on fun—costumes, prizes, noisemakers, and treats, including special holiday treats called *hamantashan* (which means "Haman's pockets").

On that holiday, the story is told of a beautiful young Judahite woman in Persia named Esther and her cousin Mordecai, who raised her as if she were his daughter. Now the king has divorced his queen, Vashti, and wants to take a new virgin bride. Esther was taken to the king's house to become part of the harem, where she was loved more than any other woman by the king who made her his queen. The villain is Haman, an arrogant advisor to the king, who plots to destroy the Judahite people because Mordecai will not bow to him.

Mordecai persuades Esther to intercede for the Judahite people with the king even though this was very dangerous for her. Esther fasts for three days to prepare herself and then goes to the King. The Judahite people were ultimately saved, and Haman was hanged on the gallows that he had prepared for Mordecai. The word Purim means "lots" and refers to the lottery that Haman used to choose the date for the massacre. When the Megillah, or scroll, of Esther is read, it is customary in the synagogue to boo, hiss, stamp feet, and rattle noisemakers whenever the name of Haman is mentioned.

Chapter 7 depicts Esther as very clever, a model of courage. She has taken the time to set the scene and has thought out what to do. As I noted, the book of Esther is well known for the fact that it does not mention God in the text. There is no real religious motivation for anything that the characters do. But there is the presence of religious practice, such as fasting, and the very character of Esther leads us to connect her courage and character to her own faith and spiritual foundation. And when it comes down to it, the book of Esther embodies the voice of God because it challenges cultural, political, social, and religious injustice.

But what do we do with those passages where God is not mentioned, where there seems to be no lesson from God, where in an odd sort of way, God is not? I suspect that God is probably not missing from this book at all; rather, God's way of moving us to be who God envisions us to be is sometimes not as obvious as wind or fire, but is instead embodied in the humanity that God shaped into the image God's Self. Esther is, then, a story of God embodied. While God is always God, perhaps this story is a reminder that God does not control the world with seemingly robotic movement, but rather continuously breathes a piece of God's Self—what Whitehead called God's "initial aim—into each thing and event in universe. Perhaps the will of God has nothing to do with fate or plans or some sort of pre-ordained destiny but is instead simply handed to us. Perhaps those places where it seems that God is not are the places where we are called to be.

Just step forward. Maybe that's the whole point. Maybe that's what the book of Esther is about—the story of one who responded to God by responding to who God envisions her to be. There is so much work to be done. God never envisioned doing it for us; otherwise, we would have been mere robots in the world and God would have instead sat motionless like some sort of divine programmer. Instead, God created time and space as we are experiencing it now and calls us to fill it with God's love grace.

James 5:13-20

The author of James expended a lot of effort telling readers that what they pray for will be received, unless prayer is undertaken with wrong motives. Whether you "suffer" or are "cheerful"—pray. If anyone is seriously ill, call upon those in official positions in the church to "pray over them" and anoint them, symbolizing the historical Jesus as the Christ of faith's healing presence and power. But here's another hiccup: while prayer made in faith may restore "health, it's not always physical or emotional health like we often imagine it, but rather a wholeness, a unity with God that might not have been there before. James also taught that prayer will restore to spiritual health any who have intentionally deviated from God's ways.

Consequently, sins should be mutually confessed to attain integrity with God, which is the meaning of "pray for one another." Then if anyone strays from integrity with God and is brought back to oneness with God through the prayer of "another" member of the community, both the one who has drifted away or the one who prays will be saved from spiritual "death" and will receive extensive forgiveness. In other words, rather than sit in judgment of each other's wrongs, we should help each other, guide each other back to a connection with God and to a wholeness of mind and spirit. In this way, the wisdom of James leaves the door open for the return of prodigal members of the community.

At the same time, the author of James seems to blur the distinction between faith and unfaith in his demand for generous openness to those who are doing powerful deeds in the name of God outside the Christian community. There is a hopefulness and an optimism about these outsiders. And there is no trace of communal imperialism

But it's not that the writer is soft on sin. The author of James strongly asserts the interconnection between Christian faith and Christian practice. He castigates the rich, the verbose, the hypocrites and the self-sufficient—anyone seeking to live their lives outside the scope of God's care. But James is hardly indifferent to believers' tendencies to wander into sin. Rather it is important to recognize that James is not eager to exclude believers when they do wander into sin. And the final, most important task for believers is to bring back those who wander away. The aim of James's generosity toward those on the margins of the community is to draw them in closer. Once drawn by the generosity of Jesus inside the circle of disciples believers must not allow each other to wander away.

This takes us back to the discipline of prayer. God whose nature is compassionate love does not need to be persuaded to care about us. The language of prayer, like the symbolic oil and the symbolic touch, engages us and God in compassionate community, a "Kingdom" or Commonwealth of God. It reminds us that we are connected to each other and that we need one other and God needs us. We are here for each other—to pray, to comfort, to cry for, to cry with, to laugh, to stand up for, to reprimand, to understand, to welcome back, and to love.

Mark 9:38-50

The disciples had previously argued about who among them is the greatest, and Jesus told them not to seek position or prestige. In these verses he rebukes them for attempting to stop an exorcist curing in his name. Jesus explains his tolerance: such a person will be slow to speak ill of him because God also works through those who are not followers of Jesus. The writer of Mark emphasizes this by using a proverb. For him or her, the "reward" is entry into the Commonwealth of God and the state of union with God awaiting him or her there.

On the other hand, putting an obstacle in the way of immature Christians ("little ones"), will lead to condemnation in our own lives. Anyone who shakes the faith of others ("causes you to stumble") is a danger to the community of faith. Then the metaphor of salt is brought into play. Salt has a multitude of symbolic meanings—it purifies, it seasons, it preserves. It is a nutrient that the body needs but cannot produce. It can remove stains and add support and buoyance. So, what does it specifically mean to be like salt, to have salt in ourselves? Perhaps we are called to be multi-faceted, to not just walk one road in the belief that we have nailed down what God requires of us, but to open ourselves to the notion that God appears when we least expect it. And we are called to be ready and do whatever it is that God calls us to do in that moment.

But we need to remember that in the ancient world salt was regarded as sacred. There were times when Roman soldiers would even receive their salaries in salt. In fact, the Latin word for "salt" is the root for "salary." For the ancients, the two most important things in life were *sol* and *sal*, sun and salt." Even today in Africa, workers often receive a portion of their pay in salt. To really understand this passage, we need to have an African view of salt. When we are told that we are salt, we are told that we are of great use and value in society. We must add flavor to everything we touch.

Yet we all know that there is often too much of a good thing. Like salt, we are not to overwhelm the world but to bring out the goodness of the world by preserving the goodness that is already there. "Being salt" means that we are called to become that embodied Presence of God in the world and for the world and, rather than making everyone and everything into what reflects our own personal image of God, we are called to season what we touch so that the flavor that is God comes through.

It's also important to note the use of the word "whoever." The disciples probably thought that Jesus meant whoever of them, but Jesus left it open—whoever—anyone. He drew the circle wider and once again the disciples missed the point. The historical Jesus never taught an "us versus them" mentality. Rather, Jesus taught that those who envision themselves aligned with him, supposedly working for the Kingdom "in his name" are kidding themselves. He was not affirming that those around him had exclusive rights to the Commonwealth of God. Rather, he was calling us to nurture all human beings in faith.

— 11 —

The Politics of Grace

Genesis 2:18–29
Psalm 26
Hebrews 1:1–4; 2:5–12
Mark 10:1–16

One of the lessons I learned from Buddhist and Daoist traditions is that there are no straight lines in nature. Nature doesn't go in a straight line, nature "wiggles." There is certainly no straight line between my head and Mark 10:1-16. Nothing in my fifty-five-year-old-marriage, nothing I know about divorce or adultery—things that are part of the history of my friendships and my experience or training in theology or biblical studies—will help me to understand with any depth the world of the historical Jesus.

But this I know: (1) Jesus was a first-century Israelite trained in the Torah, God's "Instructions" about how human beings should live in just, compassionate community. The passage thrown at Jesus by the Pharisees—Deuteronomy 24:14—is not really about divorce because it was taken for granted that a man could divorce his wife when "she finds no favor in his eyes" or when he has found some "indecency" in her. (2) Jesus lived in a cultural world of patriarchal assumptions where a man could "leave his father and mother and be joined to his wife" or divorce his wife. The concern is about male behavior. (3) Men owned women and their bodies. If a husband had sex with a woman to whom he was not married, he was not legally shaming his wife, or the woman with whom he had sex. Rather, he was bringing shame to the husband of the wife with whom he was having sex. (4) Marriage was brokered between families by the men in the families; by fathers who wanted to keep men in their marriages because offended families might start a feud that could become very bloody. Men might feel they needed to defend the honor of their families and people might be killed in the process. Furthermore, divorce was likely to injure—often physically—the wives and the women they cared for. (5) Women had no independent economic power. Provided for by father and then husband, and brothers if necessary, if a woman went from being provided for in a marriage to being on her own after a divorce, she had no guaranteed means of support. Could she go back to her family? What if her father was elderly or dead? Her options were few in such circumstances in Jesus's patriarchal culture. Chances are she would become some man's slave or prostitute. Divorce was often a male set-up for human trafficking. (6) Finally, divorce was a highly debated topic in Jesus' day. What were the appropriate grounds for divorce? Can a man divorce his wife for any reason, or only for infidelity? If divorced, could a man remarry? Could a woman? Divorce was happening all around people living in Israel and Judah. What were the specific laws or *hallakah* deciding whether or not a divorce was appropriate?

Earlier in the gospel of Mark, Jesus had a very public falling out with his family. His brothers declared him insane and his family sought to retrieve him so he wouldn't make a fool of himself and the family. In response, Jesus publicly disowned his family, a rejection that would have shocked the culture of his day. And now, a few chapters later, Jesus seems to be speaking positively of keeping families together as part of God's work in the world. He forbids divorce, completely and with no exceptions, stunning his listeners and his disciples. And after that he holds up children as emblems of discipleship.

Mark 10:1–6 is a discourse about family that seems a bit odd, particularly because Jesus devotes so much of his teaching to criticizing oppressive religious, political and economic domination systems. Such an intimate, personal message about children and divorce—especially after fracturing his own family—seems out of place, even hypocritical because Jesus has spent the majority of his time in Mark's gospel confronting systemic injustice and oppression. All of which seems to make these verses a little off topic.

But perhaps not. There is injustice and oppression everywhere, including our families. Sometimes especially in our families. The personal is political, as an old axiom goes. The family is a microcosm, often a twisted reflection, of the systems of oppression that haunt all cultures like Chinese hungry ghosts. Domestic violence against women and children—emotional or physical—is a ubiquitous example running throughout the history of human civilization. Children—the little ones that Jesus called to him—are hit daily, not just in outbursts of abuse, but also ironically as a method of instructing them not to hit, all in the name of discipline. In our own time, spousal abuse spans all sections of American society and is jarringly common. Violence, in our culture, seems to always be the answer, whether in attempting to control another country, a child, or a spouse.

This text and its synoptic parallels have received more than their fair share of attention on the recent political scene. Jesus' words about marriage have been used to shame and belittle women seeking a divorce or who have sought to marry outside the narrow definition of "male and female" (Mark 10:6). Meanwhile, his blessing of little children has become the quintessential image of a gentle and benevolent savior. And this text is really a story with two scenes. The first records Jesus' teaching about marriage. The second describes Jesus blessing a group of little children.

While many New Testament scholars link Jesus's teaching about marriage and family with the account of his blessing of children, this does not do justice either to first-century traditions about family or to the biblical texts. This is so because Jesus's concern was with human interdependency and connectedness. Following the prophetic tradition, the historical Jesus was concerned with a just, compassionate community. In the New Testament epistles there are several household codes—commonly referred to using the German term *Haustafeln*—that parallel Roman codes from the same period. A common feature in such codes is that they address three pairs of patriarchal hierarchies that are still in vogue: master and slave (or in our time, the owners of wealth and those who work for the rich and wealthy); husband and wife; parent and child. Although sometimes *Haustafeln* have been identified even when only two of the three pairs exist, Mark 10 seems like the best candidate among all the gospel accounts for a household code that can be directly attributable to the sayings of the historical Jesus. Here, Jesus addresses both married couples and children. However, three subgroups—husbands, wives, and children—made up the majority of the population in first-century Palestine, excluding only those adults who had yet to marry.

But beyond referencing this mass of the population in close proximity to each other, Mark 10 bears little resemblance to a traditional *Haustafel* for several reasons. First, the only command Jesus issues in the entire text is to his disciples, not to parents, children, or spouses: "Let the little children come to me; do not stop them" (10:14). Secondly, the whole point of household codes was to provide patriarchal standards of conduct in each relationship. This is completely lacking in Mark 10.

Thus, in spite of interpretations of Mark 10 to the contrary that imply that Jesus was restating a patriarchal moral imperative not to divorce, there is something more the author of Mark was getting at. That is, while Mark portrayed Jesus's interpretation of the Torah or "Instructions" to mean that divorce is equivalent to adultery, Jesus does not condemn divorce. Furthermore, Jesus said nothing about homosexual unions. Meanwhile, in the second scene, parents are at the sideline of the action. His real concern was the relationship between children and the Commonwealth of God as a symbolic picture of every human being's relation to this Commonwealth. And this is where I think the real connection between these two scenes—and their wisdom for our contemporary political environment—takes place.

Here's the real point: Jesus says, "Truly I tell you, whoever does not receive the kingdom of God as a little child will never enter it" (10:15). But just how do little children receive the Commonwealth of God? Perhaps with innocence and humility that lacks all pretension. But I think there is something about children and their place in the Commonwealth of God that is not reducible to virtues like innocence, vulnerability, humility, lowliness, lack of prestige, simplicity, purity, nearness to God, openness to Christ, or any other attribute we can think of. It is all this, of course, but more than this; their place in the Commonwealth of God is established simply by virtue of their being children of God.

And that's the kicker. Every child is different. Just like adults, some may be more humble than others. Some may be downright greedy. Some are incredibly bright and intelligent. Almost all are funny as a rubber crutch. But every child—every single little person who Jesus called to him that day—belongs to God. Those children, who were small enough for Jesus to scoop up in his arms and bless, still needed their parents to bring them to Jesus because they probably could not have found him on their own. The disciples weren't out of line, socially, for reproaching the children or their parents. But Jesus tells them both to stop talking for once and listen.

The historical Jesus was about much more than a set of patriarchal rules or social standards. What counts in the Commonwealth of God is simply being a child of God. Accepting and receiving the love that God has to offer as a child accepts the love of his or her parents is what Luther identified as our "calling." As adults we may have difficulty with this—being on the receiving end of a relationship, admitting our needs, admitting our failures. The children in Mark's gospel don't seem to have this hang up. Jesus blesses them, and they simply receive. Nothing else matters. And so in a world caught up in issuing patriarchal moral commands and other legalities, God beckons us, young and old, to abandon our pretensions and receive the Commonwealth of God.

Finally, Christian denominations that emphasize the sinfulness of divorce based on this text miss the heart of Jesus's teaching. The ethical force behind this teaching isn't that divorce is wrong, but that treating women as unequal to men, as possessions, is blasphemous because both men and women embody the image of God. Still, institutionalized patriarchy exists everywhere. While there are deep fractures in the glass ceiling today, it is still more difficult to be a woman than it is to be a man in every part of the world. To deny it is to be complicit in it. Women of equal skill and education command less compensation on the job. Women still do the majority of household tasks, even if they work outside their homes, even if they are the primary wage earners. Women are still viewed through sexist lenses

And it is still the wife who is typically affected disproportionately by divorce, particularly when children are involved. The husband becomes a single man. The wife becomes a single mom. It is still women and their children who suffer the most from domestic abuse or who become trapped in oppressive marriages through a husband's economic control. But the historical Jesus stood for the kind of equality that emphasized protecting all powerless and abused human beings in troubled relationships.

— 12 —

The Rich Man

Amos 5:6–7, 10–15
Psalm 12:1–15
Hebrews 4:12–16
Mark 10:17–31

I still remember the night I first read Mark's account of Jesus and the rich man. I was fourteen years old. I was at a church camp and the camp's chaplain asked me to read Mark 10:17–31 out loud at the Sunday morning service. So tucked comfortably into my sleeping bag the night before, I rehearsed reading these verses when suddenly the words, "It is easier for a camel to go through the eye of a needle than for someone who is rich to enter the kingdom of God," scared the hell out of me. I'm still not really sure why because I wasn't, and still am not, rich.

Jesus was on the move toward Jerusalem, Mark writes, when an unnamed man approached him, knelt down and asked: "Good Teacher, what must I do to inherit eternal life?" "Good Teacher!" was a very rare greeting, thrown out to flatter Jesus, and perhaps to elicit a positive response to his question. But Jesus returned no word of greeting.

The story proceeds with some tension when Jesus responds, "Why do you call me good? No one is good except God alone. You know the commandments: 'Do not kill. Do not commit adultery. Do not steal. Do not bear false witness. Do not defraud. Honor your father and mother.'" In other words, follow God's "Instructions" in the Torah. And note that Jesus substituted "do not defraud" (do not cheat someone for economic gain) for "do not covet."

Jesus' words, according to Mark, rolled over the young rich man like water off a duck's back. "Teacher," he said, "I've observed all these from my youth." *Now* according to Jewish wisdom tradition, only two men in history had followed the Torah in its entirety: Moses, and Aaron. Standing before Jesus was a young man who thought he just might be the third.

While Jesus didn't take him down a few notches, he did provide some reality therapy. Mark writes that Jesus looked at the man and "loved him." This is the only instance where Mark describes Jesus as "loving" someone. "One thing you lack," he said, "go, sell what you have, and give to the poor, and you will have treasure in heaven; and come, follow me." But something stood in the way. Another love called out the man's attention: his love of wealth and clinging to possessions stopped him cold in his tracks when he heard Jesus' instructions. He was struck, shocked, deflated, and, in the end, he sorrowfully walked away, clinging to his wealth and possessions. This is the only account in Mark in which Jesus directly asked someone to follow him, only to have that someone walk away.

The first time I read this story more years ago than I want to remember, I was scared too. But what frightened me more was when I learned that some human beings throughout history *did* sacrifice all they had when they answered the historical Jesus' call to "come, follow me."

Peter said, "Lord, we have left everything to follow you." Zacchaeus gave away most of his loot out of sheer gladness that salvation had come to his house. The early followers of the Jesus Way claimed that nothing belonged to them and sold what they had and shared everything in common so that none would be in need. And what about the poor widow who put two coins into the temple offering box? Jesus praised her for putting in everything she had to live on. How could you be happy to see a widow living on a fixed income do something so reckless? Perhaps Jesus

THE RICH MAN

understood something human beings continue to fail to grasp. And this is what scares me.

When I was a student at the Claremont School of theology, I was enrolled in a course in church history when I read about one of the first desert hermits of the Church, who lived around 250–350 CE. Antony was raised in Egypt by wealthy, Christian parents. They died when Antony was just a teenager, leaving him and his sister all their possessions. As Athanasius tells the story:

> Now it was not six months after the death of his parents, and going according to custom into the Lord's House, he communed with himself and reflected as he walked about how the Apostles left all and followed the Savior; and how they in the Acts sold their possessions and brought and laid them at the Apostle's feet for distribution to the needy, and what and how great a hope was laid up for them in heaven. Pondering over these things he entered the church, and it happened the Gospel was being read, and he heard the Lord saying to the rich man, "If thou wouldst be perfect, go and sell all that thou hast and give to the poor; and come follow Me and thou shalt have treasure in heaven." Antony, as though God had put him in mind of the Saints, and the passage had been read on his account, went out immediately from the church, and gave the possessions of his forefathers to the villagers–they were three hundred acres, productive and very fair—that they should be no more a clog upon himself and his sister. And all the rest that was movable he sold, and having got together much money he gave it to the poor, reserving a little however for his sister's sake.[1]

The next time Antony entered the church assembly he heard God say, "Don't be anxious about tomorrow." Antony could not even sit through the rest of the service before he left the church and gave his last reserve to the poor.

My professor, Jane Dempsey Douglas, told the class, "Frankly, this story frightens me to death."

Someone asked, "Why?"

1. Anatolios, ed., *Athanasius*, 75–76.

"It frightens me," she answered, "because *this man* went to church and heard the very same verses that we heard in this morning's chapel service. *Anthony* went and sold everything he had and moved into a cave in the desert in order to seek God. Today I heard the verses and I'm going home after class for a nice bowl of soup and maybe a nap after lunch."

Long ago, Jesus invited a young man to let it go, to stop clinging to the impermanent things that made him wealthy. He couldn't do it, and sorrowfully walked away. He could not trade the wild, upside-down ride of being a disciple for the security his possessions offered. And there you have it. Clinging to anything in an impermanent universe merely separates us from one another and from God as it hastens the process of our dying while simultaneously causing suffering to other human beings and the life forms with whom we share Planet Earth. This is why it's so difficult for a wealthy man or woman—any of us—to enter the Commonwealth of God on our own merits. This is why it's a good thing, as St. Paul, Augustine, and Luther discovered, that God's grace washes over all of us like a waterfall. Once we awaken to this reality, we are able to at least partially give up our clinging to the "stuff" that separates us from one another and from God.

─── 13 ───

James and John Make a Request

Job 39:1-17
Psalm 104:1-9
Hebrews 5:1-10
Mark 10:35-46

One of the remarkable facts about Christians who follow the more contemplative practices of the Christian Way lies in how they approach the world and one another. There is a quiet reserve about them coupled with a sense of hospitality and genuine submission to one another. People who observe this often mistake it for weakness, but it is a genuine way of living characterized by love and concern for the other. I suspect that this is because Christians who seriously practice faith in the historical Jesus as the Christ of faith tend to change their ways over time to more contemplative ways of life.

Job 39:1-7 and Mark 5:1-10 are centered on the theme of submission to God, a theme that is more often than not ignored in our culture of competition and egoism. The entire narrative of the Book of Job is based on a wager between God and God's opposite "adversary," "the Satan." Satan makes a wager with God that a righteous man named Job is only righteous because God has prospered him. Take away his possessions and impose hardships on Job, Satan wagers, and Job will turn against God. God takes the bet and tells Satan to take everything from Job except his life. Throughout his suffering, Job does not turn against God, but he does question why he is suffering so terribly. Finally, Job's friends offer their answers to his dilemma: Job must have offended God because God always rewards the righteous and punishes those who do not keep the Torah. But Job, who has lost his family, cattle, and land, and has suffered impoverishment and illness, rejects these conclusions. So, his friends finally offer an unsatisfactory conclusion: there is no answer except that God is "great in power and justice."

Then God himself finally answers Job out of the whirlwind in some of the most majestic poetry in the Tanak. "Where were you when I laid the foundation of the earth . . . On what were its bases sunk, or who laid its cornerstone when the morning stars sang together and all the heavenly beings shouted for joy?" And Job is swept up into the presence of the God of creation and humbly submits. Then, and only then, God restores Job's life to what it was before his wager with Satan. But note: God does not answer Job's question because there is no answer, even for God, other than just like the beauty of creation and the joys of living, undeserved suffering is just an unexplainable fact of existence. We may not like it, but we must submit to the entirety of existence, both the beautiful and creative and the painful and destructive.

A similar situation occurs in Mark 10:35–45. Jesus is confronted with a request: James and John want to join him as a power triumvirate in heaven. They presume their friendship and respect for Jesus comes with a reward, and they want to lock it in while things are going well. Jesus's response is to use their request as a teaching moment for his disciples—and each of us:

> You do not know what you are asking. Are you able to drink the cup that I drink, or be baptized with the baptism that I am baptized with?" They replied, "We are able." Then Jesus said to them, "The cup that I drink you will drink; and with the baptism with which I am baptized, you will be baptized; but to sit at my right hand or at my left is not mine to grant, but it is for those for whom it has been prepared.

The question of a place of honor was raised previously in Mark 9:33–37:

JAMES AND JOHN MAKE A REQUEST

> And they came to Capernaum; and when he was in the house he asked them, "What were you discussing on the way?" But they were silent; for on the way they had discussed with one another who was the greatest. And he sat down and called the twelve; and he said to them, "If any one would be first, he must be last of all and servant of all." And he took a child, and put him in the midst of them; and taking him in his arms, he said to them," Whoever receives one such child in my name receives me; and whoever receives me, receives not me, but him who sent me.

The question, "Who do you say that I am?" is the heart of Christian self-understanding and must be answered differently in every age. We do not live in the first century or the middle ages or the nineteenth century. Clinging to past images of Jesus and his relation to God simply will not do in a contemporary context of global religious and cultural pluralism. Not surprising, since Christians have been practicing faith within globally pluralistic contexts for two thousand years. We still haven't got it right, yet the answer is right in front of us, stalking us like a cougar after prey. According to Mark's gospel, the disciples didn't get it right even though they followed Jesus around Palestine for perhaps a year. Jesus tried to tell them, yet they didn't see the answer staring them in the face until after Jesus was killed, and then only vaguely.

In Mark 9, Jesus and the disciples have returned to his home in Capernaum after an extended journey. On the way to Caesarea Philippi, Jesus had questioned the disciples about his identity. Now on the way back home, the disciples are arguing about their own self-images—the same argument consuming James and John in Mark 10. When Jesus questions them they fall silent with embarrassment because they have been arguing about the preeminence of self—over who is the greatest. They are like fundamentalists everywhere in all religious traditions—trapped in the conventional categories of their religious systems. They, like Jesus, followed the Torah. But unlike Jesus, they clung to their culture's conventional religious Way so tightly they couldn't hear the music behind the lyrics of either the Torah or Jesus's teachings.

Like legalists and fundamentalists in all ages in all religious traditions, their path is one of fabricating verbal argumentation, of imagining a self—or a particular community of selves—exalted above others at the center of their conventional world. Their journey with Jesus had not awakened them. Instead, they saw Jesus as their ticket to glory, to selfhood exalted.

So once again Jesus instructed them about discipleship. His teaching method is to consistently subvert their notions of discipleship as assuring a preeminence of position. "He who would be first must be last," he says. To make one's self last means negating the absolute nature of one's self, of one's *persona*. This is why receiving Jesus and the one who sent him in Mark and elsewhere in other Gospel texts is exemplified as the receiving of a little child— of one who has not yet developed a strong self-image, of one who has no rank or particular importance. It is Jesus who approaches the disciples and the readers of Mark as children, with no rank or importance whatsoever. It is God who sent Jesus, who approaches the disciples and us as children, not as the romanticized image of sweet innocence, but the weakest of the weak.

Our first response as readers of Mark 9 and 10 is to disassociate ourselves from the egotistical disciples. In previous verses Jesus had just been speaking about the inevitability of his suffering and dying. And the disciples' insensitivity to Jesus's fate, combined with their crass egoism, is not a stance a reader is likely to embrace. But by a rhetorical slight-of-hand, the Markan Jesus directly addresses the reader—meaning us—through a series of paradoxical "if" and "whoever" statements: "If anyone would be first, he must be last of all and servant of all"; "whoever receives one such child in my name receives me"; "whoever receives me, receives not me but him who sent me." In other words, anyone who would follow the path of Jesus must reverse the pattern of imagined expectations and conventional understanding of religious traditions and plunge into the paradoxical world of Jesus's "doubling-back" discourse, and therein enter of the kingdom of nobodies that is the Kingdom of God.

The experience of paradox is the experience of being bracketed between seemingly incompatible but nevertheless coexisting pairs of opposites, and Mark's language about God is deeply paradoxical. Who is the "who" that sent Jesus? Why does Mark not explicitly identify God as Jesus's sender? The Markan Jesus simply says that to receive the weakest of the weak is to receive him and "him who sent me." In the same way, the voice of God speaks from the heavens at Jesus's baptism (1:11), and again from the clouds at Jesus' transfiguration (9:7). Yet Mark fails to mention just whose voice is speaking. And again, when the Markan Jesus addresses his Father in Gethsemane, no voice is heard at all. But Jesus is the son of God and our assumption that the voices Mark allows us to hear are from God is not mistaken. What *is* mistaken is that we know what this means. Not only is Jesus impossible to identify in clear definitions, God is too. What, then, could it mean to be great?

So, Job and James and John are looking at things the way we often do. They tend to see God as a Sacred Reality to be placated through worship, obedience, or honorifics, but in doing so they expect something in return. In Job's case, he gets unmitigated suffering and loss. James and John are also warned that the cup of suffering will be theirs. Okay, so who signs on for that?

The fact is that many sign up. There are Christians throughout the world who have embraced the God of the whirlwind and have accepted the cup of suffering. Desmond Tutu comes to mind as one who could have simply held the positions of Bishop of Johannesburg and then Archbishop of Capetown with its status and privilege. Instead he used those offices and his Nobel Prize to challenge the evil of apartheid, risking his own life because he knew, loved, and served a God who was above and beyond all earthly powers. And of course, there's Martin Luther King Jr.

Closer to home example for me is a friend of mine named Carl who had a successful career as a consultant. After his retirement he continued to attend his church, but he also devoted his time to finding out who the poor in his community were and bringing people together to help serve them. He created a new community where people from the neighborhood and from all walks of life met for food and fellowship. He also organized a successful program that began providing food on the weekends for children in need. Now afflicted with a serious illness, he and his wife continue to remain interested and concerned about others.

These examples of Christians who are willing to drink the cup Jesus drinks are guides to Christian living. They know what truly matters to God and they are at work in the world without care about their place or prominence in the Kingdom of God. Mark's gospel helps us focus on the question of what God expects of us, and how we are loved by God. Teddy bear hugs are replaced with leadership for true and laudable service to one another, especially the stranger, the poor, and the needy. When we behave as people of God on a mission, little else matters.

— 14 —

Blind Bartimaeus

Jeremiah 31:7–9
Psalm 34:1–8, 19–22
Hebrews 7:23–28
Mark 10:46–52

By my count, there are three distinct stories in the gospels where Jesus heals a blind man, but this is a problematic number. Sometimes the gospel writers told the same stories in different ways to make different points to different audiences. For example, in Matthew 9, Jesus heals "two blind men" by touching their eyes. In Mark 8 and John 9, Jesus heals a man at Bethsaida by picking up some dirt and spitting on it to make mud that he applied to the man's eyes. In John's version, the physical healing provokes a much longer discourse about spiritual blindness—which is an important reminder that Jesus's miracles are much more than feats of magic. Then, in a story that occurs in all three synoptic gospels there's a narrative about healing a blind man at Jericho (Mark 10; Matthew 20; and Luke 18).

There are at least thirty healing stories in the four gospels, and the persons healed are anonymous. We never learn the name of the person who was healed, except for Lazarus whom Jesus raised from the dead. But the most we ever learn is something once-removed, like "Jairus's daughter." This anonymity is another tip-off that the gospel writers were not much interested in circus-like spectacles. The miracles point beyond themselves to the more profound and mysterious identity of Jesus. He was something other than magician.

It's also worth noting that the word "miracle" does not occur in either the Tanak or the New Testament. In English, a "miracle" is an event that occurs that is contrary to the laws of nature as described by the natural sciences, whether created by God or evolved through non-theological interpretations of natural laws. In other words, "miracles are events that contradict the laws of nature that God created, which raises some rather interesting questions about God's purposes and intentions. First of all, miracles imply that the universe created by God is not dependable. Secondly, how is it that a God who is eternally creative and good grants a miraculous healing from a deadly cancer for one patient but not all. Perhaps God and the universe God creates are capricious and not dependable. So when we read about "miracles" in the Tanak and the New Testament, we are in fact reading stories about "extraordinary events"—events that are extraordinary occurrences that do not contradict the dependable universe's natural laws that God created when God created the heavens and the Earth" on the first day creation, as recorded in Genesis 1:1.

The healing story in Mark 10 is unique among the healing stores in the Gospels; it's one of thirty healing stories in which we learn the name of the person who was healed—Bartimaeus. It's a name about which scholars have spilled a lot of ink because Mark uses some interesting wordplay that points beyond the miracle story itself. "Bar-Timaeus" is a linguistic hybrid that's half Aramaic and half Greek. The author of Mark seems to have intentionally confounded his Gentile audience with a technique that he uses eight other times in this gospel by offering a parenthetical explanatory translation: "that is, the son of Timaeus." But what does *that* mean? Literally and simply, 10:46 reads, the "son of Timaeus."

Anyone who has survived an introduction to philosophy course in college should be familiar with the *Timaeus*—the title of one of Plato's dialogues and the name of its narrator. In the *Timaeus* and elsewhere, Plato famously contrasts "seeing" the mere physical world while being "blind" to Eternal Truths that ground the physical world. The *Timaeus* was the only Greek prose work that up to the third century CE every educated man or woman could be presumed to have read. Could this have included the author of Mark?

And so Bartimaeus begs Jesus, "Rabbi, I want to see!" Is the author of Mark contrasting Greek philosophy with the Judean Jesus for his Gentile audience? This is a tantalizing suggestion and I think the best conclusion is, "perhaps." This is because the name "Bartimaeus" suggests other linguistic possibilities. In simplest terms, the name combines the Aramaic *bar* (son) with the Greek *timaios* (honorable). So, Bartimaeus is a family name. He's just the son of a father named Timaeus. Or more subtly and allegorically, he's the "son of honor" or an honored person. Still other scholars point to the Aramaic or Hebrew word for "unclean" (*tame*), suggesting that Bartimaeus is the "son of the unclean."

I think it is best to combine these ideas. Bartimaeus, a down and out blind man, a poor person who begs for money, might be dishonored and marginalized by Greeks, he might be unclean to ritually clean followers of the Torah, but in Mark's telling he's a person we should honor. There's a good reason why the writer of Mark honors this dishonored man. Whereas "many people rebuked him and told him to be quiet" (10:48), trying to put him in his place, the blind Bartimaeus was insistent. Not once, but twice, he cries out, "Son of David, have mercy on me!" Longing for help and healing, the Son of Timaeus confesses that Jesus is the Son of David.

The title "Son of David" is a loaded phrase that occurs seventeen times in the gospels. It hearkens back to the very first sentence of the New Testament, where in Matthew 1:1 we read that Jesus is the "son of David." The title "Son of David" points to more than a genealogical connection. It's a confession of faith that makes a "miraculous" healing pale by comparison. Jesus is greater than Abraham. He's more than Moses or even King David. He surpasses the justly famous Plato. He's the longed-for Judean messiah mentioned in 2 Samuel 7:12–13.

The story of Bartimaeus is the last healing story in Mark. It's a transition story with a palpable sense of geographic movement.

After the healing of Bartimaeus at Jericho, Mark pivots to the triumphal entry of Jesus into Jerusalem and thus the beginning of his passion week and the fulfillment of his mission. Just before the Bartimaeus story, the disciples "were on their way up to Jerusalem" (10:32). With the healing of Bartimaeus, "they came to Jericho" (10:46). And after his healing, Bartimaeus "followed Jesus along the road" (10:52) as they "approached Jerusalem and came to Bethpage and Bethany at the Mount of Olives" (11:1).

As with virtually all the characters in the gospels, we never hear about Bartimaeus again. But with Mark's description of how he followed Jesus those seventeen miles from Jericho to Jerusalem, I like to picture the Son of Timaeus conversing with the Son of David while walking with him to the City of David. Bartimaeus invites us to the same journey of "following Jesus on the way," and to the same confession, "Jesus, Son of David, have mercy on me!"

— 15 —

Reformation Day

Jeremiah 31:31–34
Romans 3:19–28
John 8:31–36

The event that radically changed the course of Martin Luther's life—and is the beginning of the Protestant Reformation—took place near Stotterheim, Germany, on July 2, 1505. Luther had recently completed his master's degree and started his law studies at the University of Erfurt. On his way back to Erfurt, after having visited his parents, he was caught in a terrible thunderstorm. Lightning struck near him, and he was thrown to the ground by the air pressure. It scared him witless, and at that moment he called to Saint Anne and declared, "I will become a monk!" Luther often commented on this event later and the evidence is that he played with the idea of becoming a monk even before the storm scared him witless. Facing his father's disgust and anger—because he wanted his son to study law—Luther honored his solemn promise. He had one last party with university friends on July 16, and the next day he entered the Black Monastery in Erfurt to become an Augustinian friar.

What drove Luther to the monastic life was the conviction that he along with all human beings were sinners who deserved only God's angry wrath and punishment. At this time in his life, "salvation" meant eternal life after death in God's paradise, but this had to be earned by what St. Paul and Augustine called "works," meaning structuring one's life according to God commandments and participation in the Catholic Church's sacramental system, particularly confession and penance. Then, and only perhaps, God would extend mercy and forgive a serious penitent's sins and grant eternal life. But the destiny of most repentant human beings was a state of after-life existence called "purgatory," where one painfully suffered for one's sins so that God's justice could be satisfied, after which God would be merciful and finally grant eternal life. At the time, Luther agreed with fifteenth-century Roman Catholic theology: only the "saints" revered by Christians entered eternal life at death. The vast majority of human beings are headed for God's painful payback for human sinfulness in purgatory, while unredeemable persons are headed for the eternal punishment of hell.

Luther struggled like a man possessed to earn God's favor. But no matter how hard he tried, no matter how long he prayed, studied, or submitted to the ascetic disciplines of enclosed Augustinian friars, no matter how hard he tried to follow the instruction of his spiritual director, Johann Staupitz (1460–1524), Luther thought he was a failed, sinful human being who would never experience God's saving grace—even as Staupitz told Luther, "God isn't angry with you; you're angry with God."

His sense of failure haunted him like a Chinese hungry ghost until one day, while reading Paul's epistle to the Romans, he had an insight that hit him like a ton of bricks. The verse that stopped him cold and seared into his mind is Romans 3:28: "For we hold that a person is justified by faith apart from works prescribed by the law." Luther interpreted this verse as "justification by faith through grace alone," even though, as my Roman Catholic friends correctly point out, the word "alone" does not occur in the original Greek text of verse 28. But Luther was one of the finest biblical scholars of his day and knew by experience that all translations are interpretations based on the experiences of the translator. I personally think Luther's translation is spot on because it encompassed his sense of failure as an Augustinian friar. And it wasn't long after Romans 3:28 radically altered his theological vision that he left the monastery and built a movement seeking to reform late medieval Christian faith and practice.

Everything in the Protestant Reformation is built on Romans 3:28. Here's why.

At the heart of the Protestant Reformation is the affirmation *ecclesia semper reformands, semper reformanda* ("the church is always reformed, always reforming"). While many Christians in Luther's time as well as today often cling to the relics of past doctrine, preferring the stability of human constructs to the dynamic movements of a living God, faithfulness to the Reformation is a matter of spirit and experience along with willingness to constantly share one's faith in new and creative ways. That is to say, Reformation faith is forward-looking rather than backward-looking, evolving rather than static, at home in this world rather than in a previous age or a heavenly realm or an imaginary future.

Accordingly, as they sought to articulate their faith, the Lutherans affirmed, and still do, five *solas* ("alone")—*sola scriptura, sola fides, sola gratia, solus Christus, soli Deo Gloria*. These *solas* expressed the contours of the Lutheran tradition of the Reformation while not narrowly defining the meaning of faith. That is, to be faithful to the Reformed tradition each of these *solas* must be constantly updated to respond to God's call in a constantly changing universe. In the following paragraphs, I propose to describe what these *solas* might mean in a global, postmodern, scientific, pluralistic age. My argument assumes that in building upon and going beyond the original insights of Luther, we are most connected to the Protestant Reformation.

Sola Scriptura. Scripture alone is the ultimate source of authority for Protestants. But narrowly defined, this leads to an unimaginative, backward-looking, culture-hating, and intolerant literalism quite different than what the Reformers intended. Scripture is central to faith, but it can be never become an idol. We cannot substitute biblical infallibility for papal infallibility. We cannot worship words or let them get in the way of the Living Word, incarnate in Jesus Christ or in the actual words of the biblical text. Just as God's mercies are new every morning, faithfulness to Scripture means challenging Scripture when it deviates from God's graceful presence. Luther had doubts about the epistle of James, describing it as an "epistle of straw." While Luther certainly missed the point of James as a text joining works with grace, rather than a works-centered text, Luther clearly saw Scripture as relative and subject to reformation whenever the occasion arises.

This means that Christians must see the biblical text as an evolving document. In our time, this entails rejecting passages that promote violence and the objectification of women, "non-believers," and the LGBT community. We must, with Luther and other Reformers, look for the "Word" of grace within the words of scripture. A graceful reading of scripture opens us to experiencing divine wisdom in science, medicine, literature, and non-Christian religious Ways. Scripture is always an open door, never a closed door.

Sola Fides. Though faith always has an "in spite of" element, faith is not affirming things we know to be untrue scientifically, ethically, or theologically. As Luther asserted, faith is a lively, reckless confidence in the grace of God. Faith involves trust and relationship, grounded in experience, study, and community. But faith is never reducible to doctrines and/or creeds. Faith is not strict adherence to doctrines, with death and damnation awaiting all who doubt or disbelieve; rather, faith involves openness to experiencing the Sacred in all its manifestations, even in the unfamiliar and unexpected.

Today, faith involves experiencing and trusting God's wisdom in the witness of persons of other faith traditions, seekers, agnostics, and atheists. It involves openness to following divine guidance wherever it takes us, even beyond the precincts of Christian tradition. It is an act of faith to affirm the truths of the Christian Way while embracing divine wisdom broadcast in other religious Ways. Our truths do not depend on their falsehoods, but on an ongoing trust in God's evolving grace and wisdom reflected in human finitude and imperfection. In the spirit of author Madeleine L'Engle, when she was asked if she believed in God without any doubts, faith asserts, "I believe in God with all my doubts." "Doubting Thomas," not the nondoubting fundamentalist, is the true follower of Christian faith.

Sola Gratia. Everything is about grace. We receive God's love regardless of our current spiritual or ethical state. Though unmerited, grace is not "in spite of" of who we are, but "because of" who God is. Grace does not diminish the human enterprise, but invites us to live abundantly, fully, and creatively. Though grace is universal, it is not unilateral or uniform. Grace works uniquely within each person. Grace does not depend on our works; we receive it, rather than earn it. Still, the shape of grace is personal and depends on our relationship to God and to one another.

Grace calls us to action, bringing forth our goodness and inviting us to be God's partners in healing the earth.

Though the first Protestant Reformers scorned Pelagius due to their uncritical acceptance of Augustine's diatribes against the Celtic theologian, today's Reformers can learn much from Pelagius. In fact, we need both Augustine and Pelagius in the formation of a holistic faith: unstoppable grace comes to us, accepting and empowering us in all our brokenness; grace awakens our essential goodness and invites us to be partners in God's mission.

God's sovereignty does not depend on our passivity. Rather, our receptivity to grace leads to action and mission. The more complete our responses to grace, the more our lives experience processes of creative transformation. God does not compete with us in power; rather God's power enhances our creativity, freedom, and power to change the world. On this point, Whiteheadian process theologians are in agreement with the Reformation.

Solus Christus. Christ alone is the rock of our relationship to God. While some Christians read this in terms of "no salvation outside the church" or outside a specific doctrinal affirmation of faith, my suggestion is that "Christ alone" points to the interplay of universality and diversity. Grace is not grace if it is limited to adherence to a particular doctrinal understanding or religious tradition. Christ liberates us to seek truth and healing wherever they are found, whether in the laboratory, hospital, library, or other faith traditions. Grace allows us to pursue truth in whatever form it assumes. Grace opens the doors of revelation to all creation, giving hospitality and inspiration to human beings everywhere at all times and in all places.

Soli Deo Gloria. God's glory alone is the center of our lives and all creation. God is the heart of reality, in whom we live and move and have our being. To affirm God's glory is to rejoice in the wonder of life and the beauty of our own lives. God's glory transforms and enlivens us and opens us—with Isaiah—to discover that "the whole earth is filled with God's glory." A relational, non-competitive God, defined by grace and love, seeks our abundant life. As a wise church father once proclaimed, the glory of God is a human being fully alive.

A God of grace and glory moves through every cell, every molecule of the universe, every life form, enlivening, enlightening, and energizing—a theological perspective known as "panentheism." God's ultimate concern is our "salvation"—our wholeness and healing—and in the transformation of this good earth so that it might reflect God's aim at beauty, truth, goodness, and justice. We honor God by following the counsel of Mother Teresa, "to do something beautiful for God." We give glory to God by living in a sacramental way, seeing the whole world as filled with God's grace and sharing in God's pathways of salvation for all creation. But, as descendants of the Reformation, we must constantly reform our faith, updating it constantly, dialoging with other religious Ways, and committing ourselves to a justice-seeking, world-affirming, beauty-creating Way of life.

16

All Sinners and Saints Day

Isaiah 25:6–9
Psalm 24
Revelation 21:1–6a
John 16:32–44

I prefer thinking of "All Saints Day" as "All Sinners and Saints Day."[1] One of the central themes in Martin Luther's theology that led to his excommunication from the Roman Catholic Church in the fifteenth century was that human beings are *simul justus et peccator*, meaning "simultaneously saints and sinners." To this day, a saint in the Catholic tradition is someone whose life was so extraordinary that after critical examination by the papal hierarchy, that person is declared a conduit through whom God's grace flows into people's lives. Saints are "venerated," rather than worshipped, since only God may be worshipped. One of the requirements for sainthood is that devout persons receive miracles from persons nominated for sainthood. In this way, saints are understood to be mediators between human beings and God. In Luther's day, most people venerated saints rather than praying directly to God. Luther's teaching of *simul et justus peccator* means that God is directly related to human beings—indeed, to all life—without the need for saintly go-betweens.

---

1. See Boltz-Weber, *Accidental Saints*. Nadia Bolz-Weber is the founding pastor of House for All Sinners and Saints in Denver, Colorado.

In the Protestant, and particularly the Lutheran tradition, All Saints and Sinners day is a liturgical celebration of those of us who have died and are now in a state of existence different from the one we experience while alive called "eternal life." In other words, our family members, friends, and people we don't know are now the "saints" whose lives we celebrate. Somehow, the dead are interconnected with the living. I first experienced this interconnection while visiting European churches and cathedrals, which are typically surrounded by huge cemeteries with gravestones dating back centuries. Often baptisms and wedding receptions are held in these cemeteries. Those who have died are regarded as members of the congregation, which I think they are.

But here's my hiccup: I'm not sure what death is even though I am surrounded by it. After all, life must eat life to survive. But before we can know anything, we must first experience what we know, and by the time we experience *our* deaths, it may be too late to know—if the natural sciences are correct in the conclusion that death means the end of lived existence—period! Freeman Dyson notes something similar in the concluding paragraphs of his *Origins of Life*:

> There is a sloppiness to life in which life must be able to tolerate error in order to be robust. Novelty happens at the edge of chaos, so that if something is too stable, too robust it's just rigid, and nothing new can evolve. Its on that edge, in that sloppy region where openness is joined to preservation that life happens. This chaotic region, where all living things must live in order to live at all, is necessarily a dangerous place. But not because God is careless or incompetent. It's just the cost for the fruitfulness of life.[2]

I think something like this idea lies behind St. Paul's portrayal of Jesus as the Christ:

> He is the image of the invisible God, the first born of all creation, for in him all things were created, in heaven and on earth, visible and invisible . . . he is the beginning,

2. Dyson, *Origins of Life*.

the first born from the dead, that in everything he might be permanent. For in him all the fulness of God was pleased to dwell, and through him to reconcile himself to all things, whether in earth or in heaven. (Colossians 1:15–20)

Or as my theology professor, John B. Cobb Jr., interprets the defining experience of faith:

> The structure of experience with Christ which is bound up with hope in history is that of dying and rising. Each moment, as soon as it is realized, itself perishes or dies. The new moment lives only as it finds some novel possibility that is its own, appropriate to its own, appropriate to the unique situation, and worthy of realization in its own right. Living from our past instead is not a real option. If we seek life by clinging to past realizations, we do not live at all. It is only a question of the pace of death. The one who holds onto the past and repeats is does not enliven the past but only joins it in death. However, the one who turns from the past in openness to the new finds the past restored and revitalized . . . It is when we think new thoughts that our past thinking remains a vital contributing element, not when we endlessly repeat ourselves or try to defend what we thought in the past.[3]

In other words, it is by dying that we live—the whole point celebrated at All Saints and Sinners Day. Whatever redemption is, it encompasses more than humanity, past, present, or future; redemption encompasses the whole natural order, every thing and event caught in the field of space-time since the first instant of the Big Bang until the physical processes of this universe finally play out trillions of years into the future. For, as someone writing in Saint Paul's name put it, "God was in Christ reconciling the world to God's self" (2 Corinhtians 5:19) The deepest meaning of the universe made visible in the cemeteries surrounding European Cathedrals, the meaning of fourteen billion years of evolution and beyond, is that all of nature—every thing and event caught in the field of space-time, has

---

3. Cobb, *Christ in a Pluralistic Age*, 243.

been, is now, and always will be united to God. Nothing is left out that can be included. Absolutely nothing.

So, All Saints and Sinners Day is a day set aside in the church year to remember the saints. But not just the ones who have died since it is technically *All* Saints and Sinners Day, and not just *Some* Saints and Sinners Day. To be clear, this isn't like a cult of saints. We don't need special saints to intercede for us because God listens to them more since they were just basically better Christians than we. What we celebrate when we celebrate All Saints and Sinners Day is not the superhuman faith and power of a select few. We celebrate God's ability to use flawed people to do divine things. We celebrate all on whom God has acted in baptism, sealing them, as Ephesians says, with the mark of the promised Holy Spirit. We celebrate the fact that God creates faith in God's people through ordinary acts of love. We celebrate that we have in all who've gone before us what St Paul calls a great cloud of witnesses and that the faithful departed are as much the body of Christ as we are.

It is quite a thing, really, that we are so interdependent, connected by so much faith, so many stories, so much divine love. Especially in this day and age of alienation and trying to find community and belonging in smaller and smaller ways. I mean, I may think that the basis of my being connected to other people is in having theology or political beliefs or denominational affiliation or neighborhood or musical taste or Facebook groups in common. But none of that is what connects me to the Body of Christ. What connects me to the body of Christ is not my piety or good works or theological beliefs. It's God. A God who gathers up all things and events into the Commonwealth of God.

Yet it is important to remember that all of us are simultaneously faithful and deeply flawed saints. I think of Mary Magdalene and Peter the fisherman and the other eleven disciples. I love thinking about St. Frances, Mother Teresa, and Martin Luther King Jr. Whenever I remember my father and mother, my brother, Bill, my father's eldest brother, Fred, my wife's mother and father, I always smile and grieve simultaneously. And I thank God for gathering so many into the church eternal, some of whom still light our own paths. Many of us attend services on All Saints and Sinners Sunday to honor loved ones who have died. Our hearts will be heavy with the loss of someone we love, people who we'd frankly rather still have with us as living persons and not as a photo on a white table at church the first Sunday of November. We'd rather be standing behind them in line for communion than adding them to the litany of saints.

But we will speak the names of those who have departed this world since the last All Saints and Sinners Day—expectedly, unexpectedly, peacefully, violently. And all of them now taken into the embrace of the God from whom they came in the first place, because God somehow gathers us all up into the divine love of Christ and makes us a body both now and in the life to come. Even those whose names are eventually forgotten are always and forever held in the light of God in glory. Because while death is a wrenching painful reality to us, it is also so with God.

Not that God is impervious to the pain of death. The historical Jesus had real friends who died, and he stood outside the tomb of Lazarus and wept. And then, of course, he raised Lazarus from the grave—as though before Jesus could defeat death he needed to first gave it a really good slap in the face. Jesus was so moved by God's compassion and love for those who others rejected that he went to a cross we built for him, and then descended to the dead as though to say to us "even here I will find you and not let you go," because death has no sting—death is rendered meaningless to a God of resurrection. And lest we forget, it is a God of resurrection that faithful Christians anticipate.

— 17 —

The Prophetic Widow

Ruth 3:1–5; 4:13–17
or 1ˢᵗ Kings 17:8–16
Psalm 127 or Psalm 146
Hebrews 9:24–28
Mark 12:38–44

"The Widow's Mite" is a classic Gospel story and a standard text for churches during Stewardship Season. There are not many Christians who have not heard the story of a nameless widow who slips quietly into the Temple, drops her meager offering into the treasury, and slips away. I mean, who hasn't squirmed when a pastor saddles the story to his or her stewardship sermon: "If a poor widow can give her sacrificial bit for the Lord's work, how can we—so comfortably wealthy in comparison—not give much, *much* more?"

I have to admit that I've squirmed too, but not because the question critiques giving. I squirm because this woman's "mite" haunts me; her story as recounted in Mark has a very hard edge and I don't want it reduced to a moral teaching or exploited for the sake of capital campaigns and annual budgets. I wish I knew her name. I wish I knew for certain that her real-life fierceness exceeded the piety conventional Christians impose on her. And I hope she died with dignity. Yes, she died probably days after she dropped her two coins into the Temple treasury, because here is what Jesus is reported to have said as she left the Temple: "She out of her poverty has put in everything she had, all she had to live on." And as far as I can tell from reading the Gospels, Jesus wasn't given to exaggeration. She was an impoverished widow in first-century Palestine, a woman living on the margins of her society. She had no safety net. No husband to advocate for her, no pension upon which to draw, no social status behind which to hide. She was vulnerable in every way that mattered. And if I'm getting the timing right, Jesus died four days after the events in this story. I wonder if the widow did, too.

Here's what makes me squirm: what does it mean to applaud a destitute woman who gave her last two cents to the Temple, and then slipped away to starve? Is this really a story of selflessness? Should we cheer or weep? Mark prefaces the story of the widow within an account of Jesus sharply denouncing the religious leaders of his day for their greed, pretentiousness, and exploitation of the poor. "Beware of the scribes," Jesus tells his followers. "They devour widow's houses and for the sake of appearance say long prayers." In other words, their piety is a sham and the religious institution they govern is corrupt because it is not in any way reflective of the God the psalmist calls, "a Father of orphans and protector of widows" (Psalm 146:9).

In fact, in the days leading up to the widow's gift, Jesus offered one scathing critique after another of the economic and political exploitation he witnessed all around him. He made a mockery of Roman pomp and circumstances when he processed into Jerusalem on the back of jackass. He cleansed the temple's money changing industry with a whip. He refused to answer the chief priests, scribes, and elders when they demanded to know the source of his authority. He confounded religious leaders on taxes, indicted them with a scathing parable about a vineyard and a murdered son, defeated them on the question of resurrection, and bewildered them with riddles about his Davidic ancestry. So why on earth would he turn around and praise a woman for endangering her already endangered life to support an institution he condemned?

The simple answer is, he doesn't. Centuries of stewardship sermons notwithstanding, Jesus doesn't commend the widow, never applauds her self-sacrifice, or invites us to follow in her footsteps. He simply noticed her and tells his disciples to notice her, too. This is the moment in the story when I'd give anything to hear the tone in Jesus's voice. What did it mean to him, mere seconds after he'd described the temple leaders as devourers of widows' houses, to witness a widow being devoured? And worse, participating in her own devouring? And here's a telling postlude: immediately after the widow leaves the temple, Jesus leaves, too, and as he does, an awed disciple invites Jesus to admire the Temple's mammoth stones and impressive buildings. Jesus' response is quick and cutting: "Not one of these stones will be left upon another; all will be thrown down."

I wonder if the widow was still on Jesus's mind as he predicted the destruction of the Temple. He had just watched a trusting woman give her all to an indefensible institution, one that refused to protect the poor. No edifice steeped in such injustice will stand. So back to my earlier question: should we cheer or weep in the face of this story? Or should faithful Christians call out any form of religiosity that manipulates the vulnerable into self-harm and self-destruction?

Jesus *noticed* the widow. He saw that everyone else was too busy, too grand, too spiritual, and too self-absorbed to notice. For me, this is the only redemptive part of the story—that Jesus's eyes were ever on the small, the insignificant, the hidden.

What did Jesus notice? I don't know for sure, but I'll hazard some guesses. I think he noticed the widow's courage. I imagine it took quite a bit of courage for her to make her gift alongside the rich with their fistfuls of coins. Even more courage to allow the last scraps of her security to fall out of her palms. And more still to swallow panic, swallow desperation, swallow the human desire to cling to life no matter what—and face her end with hope. I also think Jesus noticed her dignity. Surely, she had to steel herself when widowhood rendered her worthless and "expendable" in the temple she loved. Surely, she trusted, in the face of all the evidence piled up around her, that her tiny gift had value in God's eyes. And finally, I think Jesus noticed her vocation. Whether she knew it or not, the widow's action in the temple that day was prophetic. She was a prophet in the sense that her costly offering amounted to a denunciation of injustice and corruption. Without speaking a word, she spoke God's Word in the ancient tradition of Isaiah, Elijah, Jeremiah, and other prophets. But she was also prophetic in a Messianic sense because her self-sacrifice prefigured Jesus's self-sacrifice. Perhaps what Jesus noticed was kinship. Her story mirroring his. The widow gave everything she had to serve a world so broken, it killed her. Days later, Jesus gave everything he had to redeem, restore, and renew that world, and, the world killed him too.

— 18 —

Whom Shall We Trust?

> Daniel 12:1–3
> 1 Samuel 2:1–10
> Psalm 113
> Hebrews 10:11–14, (15–18), 19–25
> Mark 3:1–8

Apocalyptic themes, each expressed in their own specific historical contexts, run in each of these texts. Apocalyptic themes focus on the ultimate destiny of the world when whole communities are experiencing political, military, economic, and religious domination systems of oppression—systems controlled by the rich and powerful who, in the words of the prophet Amos, graze off the majority of human beings like the rich women he calls "the cows of Bashan" (Amos 4:1–3). Apocalyptic literature is meant to encourage oppressed people by pointing to a better, immediate future in process of being established by God—a future free from war, violence, and oppression by domination systems, a near time when, in the words of Micah, human beings will live in solidarity of community founded on justice and compassion (Micah 6:6–8).

First, Daniel 12:1–3, whose context is the oppressive systems of Greek domination over Judah and the cooperation of the Temple leadership with the Greek authorities. One of the arguments that atheists often use to demonstrate the unlikelihood of God's existence is the reality of injustice in the world. This experience is nothing new. It was certainly the reality faced by the majority of people living in Daniel's time, roughly the second century BCE. It is certainly the reality the vast majority of human beings face now. Those who are poor and weak suffer the most, while the rich suffer very little. Furthermore, those who happened to be born in countries with few financial resources are more likely to suffer from war or famine than those born in rich countries. In a just world, so the argument goes, the good would be rewarded and the wicked would be punished. The observation that the world does not operate in this manner is central to the argument of the book of Job. As Job observes, the wicked often prosper and the righteous suffer, in contrast to the sentiment "I've never seen the righteous forsaken" (Psalm 37:25)

Of course, this is the problem of undeserved suffering: If God is all powerful and good, and rewards those who follow his laws, then why is it that so many good and Godfearing people experience suffering that is neither deserved nor earned by anything they have done or not done? Is there no resolution to this problem? Is God really unjust? Does God give a damn? Does God exist?

Another solution to this problem appears in Daniel 12:1–3. Daniel is the latest book of the Tanak. The book of Daniel's reality therapy points out that those who are faithful to God often suffer in this life, and thus life is indeed unfair. But the problem disappears when the next life is taken into account, a life in which the righteous truly are rewarded and the wicked truly are punished. This is also the solution that the New Testament writers, as well as classical Judaism and Islam, adopted. But it too contains inherent problems. Is this not a theology of divine child abuse? And who is completely righteous? No one. Who is completely wicked? Again, no one—with the possible exception of Adolf Hitler. Christians, especially Protestants, attempt to skirt this issue by substituting Christ's righteousness for the righteousness of the individual believer, as Paul advocates. But such theologies of divine child abuse raise other issues. What about the person who has never heard of Christ, or who hasn't had a real opportunity to believe in Christ? What about those who lived before the historical Jesus? Is eternal punishment a just sentence for temporal sin? These and other questions continue to be debated by people of faith, and perhaps they will continue to be debated. One thing Daniel teaches us is that regardless of how we resolve the God-theodicy paradox, it is God who, when all is said and done, takes care of those who respond with all the faith they can muster in hard times.

The context of First Samuel is Israel's war against the Philistines, David's capture of Jerusalem from the Jebusites, bringing the Arc of the Covenant to Jerusalem, and David's anointing as the second king of the Israelites. The poem in First Samuel 2:1–10 illustrates how people in ancient times—as well as people today—will readily make political choices that are contrary to their own best interests. I'm not thinking about those few who are rich who advocate lower estate taxes, based on the principle that inheriting excessive wealth does not violate justice. Instead, I'm thinking about the middle class and the poor who vote for candidates who vow to reduce the tax burden on the rich as they shift the economic burden down the socioeconomic ladder.

I can think of only two reasons why people might vote against their own economic self-interest. The first reason is that they truly believe that the adjustments to the tax code advocated by their candidates are fair. I doubt, however, that this is the case with the vast majority of middle and lower-class people who vote in this manner. The second reason, which I think predominates in the mind of those who vote this way, is that they hope one day to be rich so that they too might enjoy the benefits of a lowered tax burden. They idolize the rich, and they fantasize about being rich, so they vote for politicians who favor the rich, on the off chance that they may someday benefit. Hannah's song offers a shrill wakeup call to this kind of thinking. God, she says, doesn't side with the rich, but with the poor. God lifts up the poor and needy while bringing down those who are rich and powerful. Desiring membership in the club of the rich is like trying to join a yacht club on the *Titanic*. There's just no future in it. Which brings me to Hebrews 10:11–14 (15–18), 19–25, the historical context of which is Christian and Judean oppression by the harsh domination systems of the Roman empire.

"Whenever we argue, you always get historical," I once said (in jest) to my wife, Regina.

"You mean hysterical, honey," she replied.

"No, I mean historical. You always bring up everything I've done wrong in the past."

This is exactly how we often face the issue of sin and forgiveness. We say that we forgive those who have wronged us in some way, but if they wrong us again, or if we need justification for wronging them, we have no qualms about dredging up old complaints. Similarly, we often have a hard time forgiving ourselves as we imagine that since we are unable to forget the wrongs done to us, God is similarly unable to forgive and forget. However, the passage in Hebrews says precisely, "Where there is forgiveness of these [sins], there is no longer any offering for sin."

Of course, it is true that some sins are harder to forgive than others. If you feel that you've been grievously wronged, it's much harder to forgive that person who sinned against you than if the wrong was nothing more than a slight. There are also certain classes of sin that we seem to have a hard time forgiving. Many conservative churches find it much easier to admit a person to full fellowship who has committed armed robbery, drug dealing, or even murder than to admit a member of the LGBT to their communities. In many churches, divorce is the unpardonable sin, regardless of the circumstances or the passing of time.

But before we get on our high horse and condemn the sin of another person, offering little recourse in the way of forgiveness, it is always a good idea to remember our own sins, and the fact that God has forgiven us. When I adopt this approach myself, I find that I have a hard time being too judgmental of the sins of others, particularly when the person who has sinned has asked forgiveness. If we expect God to forgive our sins permanently, we must be willing to do the same for others. "Forgive us our trespasses, as we forgive those who trespass against us," as the Lord's Prayer instructs.

Finally, Mark 13:1–8, written shortly after the Romans invaded Judah and destroyed the Temple in 70 CE, a war that brought horrible suffering to both the Judean and Christian communities in Palestine and throughout the Roman empire. As I was reading this text, the memory of the day Dick Cheney became vice president in 2001 popped into my mind. One of the first things he did was call on the leaders of the energy industry for a secret sit-down to discuss the Bush administration's energy policy. One of the companies represented at the table was Enron, the poster child for growth in the industry. Kenneth Lay and Jeffrey Skilling had put together a company that was one of the biggest on Wall Street, and people everywhere wanted to emulate their success. The Houston Astros even named their new stadium Enron Field. Then the bottom fell out. It turned out that the superstructure upon which Enron was built was little more than a glorified pyramid scheme. They borrowed money from one of their companies to make their other companies look good on paper, but eventually their accounting sleight of hand caught up with them, and Enron fell to pieces. President George W. Bush pretended that he didn't even know Kenneth Lay, and the Astros erased Enron from their stadium and replaced it with a Minute Maid logo.

People are often impressed by the wrong things. Mark's gospel tells us that Jesus's disciples were impressed with the Jerusalem temple, but Jesus told them not to put so much emphasis on things that that pass away. Today, all that remains of the temple that the Romans destroyed in 70 CE is the western wall. The great pyramids of Central America were marvelous feats of engineering, but when the Mayan civilization fell, the jungle took over the pyramids. The World Trade Center towers were tall and majestic, but they were destroyed on a single, terrible September morning. It's tempting to put our trust in institutions or structures that people have built, but none of which will last. The Great Wall of China failed to keep the Mongols out, just as Hadrian's Wall failed to keep the Scotts out. Similarly, the wall the Israelis are now building through the middle of Palestinian territory will not bring peace to the Israel, nor will the wall that Donald Trump is seeking to build on the Mexican border solve US immigration problems. Our trust should not be in buildings or walls or corporations or defense systems; our trust should only be in God, and in the strategies that Jesus proclaimed: peacemaking, loving one's enemies, and forgiving those who have wronged us.

— 19 —

"What Is Truth"

Second Samuel 23-1-7
Psalm 132:1-12
Revelation 1:4b-8
John 18:33-37

I once did some Google searches on the meaning of "truth." Here are the titles of articles that popped up most often: "The Death of Truth," "The Assault on Truth," "Notes on Falsehood," "Our Post-Truth World." Although these articles focused on contemporary American politics, their conclusions reached beyond politics to a more sinister and existential reality: we live in an Age of Untruth. Politics notwithstanding, we are steeped in a culture of blatant lies, sly exaggerations, doctored images, wild conspiracy theories, and fake news. Objective facts, for all intents and purposes, no longer matter to the vast majority of contemporary human beings. I suspect this was true for the majority of human beings in past history as well. Truth is falsehood, falsehood is true, and anything can mean anything.

What does this sobering situation have to do with that part of the lectionary called, "The Season of Pentecost?" The final Sunday of Pentecost is a liturgical hinge between the long "Season of Pentecost," and the beginning of Advent. Which means this "hinge" is primarily a reflection on the meaning of Christ's reign over the Church, the world, and the lives of faithful Christians. What kind of "king" is the historical Jesus confessed to be

"WHAT IS TRUTH"

the Christ of Faith? What does his rule look and feel like? What does it mean to live and thrive under his kingship? If Jesus is king, then who or what is *not*?

In reflecting on this question, the lectionary readings offer a counter portrayal of Jesus' kingship and Jesus' teaching about the Commonwealth of God. First, Jesus is not portrayed as having conventional kingly power. Instead, the Gospel of John offers us a picture of the historical Jesus at his physical and emotional worst: arrested, disheveled, harassed, hungry, abandoned, sleep-deprived—and standing before the notoriously cruel Pontius Pilate for questioning. If I were going to write Jesus into a kingly scene, this would *not* be the one I'd write. But if there is any story about Jesus that can smack all smugness out of us—all arrogance, all gleefulness, all scorn—surely this one *has* to be it. Our "king" is an arrested, falsely accused criminal. A dead man walking. His chosen path is one of humility, surrender, brokenness, and loss.

But the question is, what does any of this have to do with our current crisis of truth and untruth? Consider, for example, the exchange that takes place between Jesus and Pilate: "Are you a king?" Pilate asks Jesus repeatedly, annoyed, perhaps, that a bedraggled peasant is taking up his valuable time on a tense and busy weekend. "*You* say that I am a king," Jesus answers cryptically, implying that Pilate's question is the wrong one because Pilate's assumptions about power and kingship are irrelevant to what is happening before his eyes. Then Jesus continues: "For this I came into the world, to testify to the truth. Everyone who belongs to the truth listens to my voice."

Then Pilate asks a question that has haunted human beings since our Neanderthal ancestors painted the shapes of animals in deep caves in Lascaux, France, forty-thousand years ago: "What is truth?" I have no idea if Pilate even really asked this question. But it doesn't matter because Jesus offers no verbal response. He doesn't engage Pilate in the sort of philosophical dialogue that would have made Plato or Aristotle smile. Instead, his response is embodied within his whole life, as if to say, "You're looking at it." "You're *looking* at the truth. I am the truth." In other words, truth isn't an instrument, a weapon, or a slogan we can smack on a bumper sticker or use as a political slogan or used to sell cheap stuff in a television add. The truth *is* the historical Jesus, meaning the life of Jesus, the way of Jesus, the love of Jesus, and the death of Jesus. He himself is a complex embodiment of truth.

What can this possibly mean in our contemporary post-truth era? What does it mean to "belong to the truth" in a culture that increasingly denies truth's validity? Perhaps most importantly, how can we bear witness to embodied truth, complex truth, truth as an Incarnation story of birth and life and death and resurrection, in a world that prefers soundbites, tweets, and clever New Yorker cartoons?

The more I reflect on this Gospel passage, it seems to me that one of the most urgent tasks facing the Church is forging a robust but gracious, urgent but respectful, relationship to the Truth. If Jesus came to testify to the truth, if he *is* the truth, what does loyalty to the historical Jesus Christians confess to be the Christ of faith look like here and now? Perhaps something like this: if Truth is king, then "fake news" is not. If Truth is king, then self-deception—however expedient or attractive—is not. If Truth is king, then lazy relativism is not. If Truth is king, then distorting inconvenient facts for our own political, racial, social, cultural, religious, or economic comfort, is not.

As I write this essay, I'm painfully aware of the Church's long and miserable tradition of using "the truth" to consolidate and abuse its own power. Over the centuries, Christians have excelled at using "truth" to colonize, enslave, reject, and dehumanize those we conveniently call "the Other." But that's not the kind of truth to which Jesus called his followers to embody. The truth Jesus embodied in his life, death, and resurrection is not instrumental or self-aggrandizing. It does not bolster his own power and authority. Quite the opposite—it humbled him. It broke him. It killed him. And as far as I can tell, Jesus's embodiment of truth did not privilege any version of truth that sidesteps humility, surrender, and sacrificial love. He did not secure his own prosperity at the expense of other people. He did not allow religious teaching and practices to justify unjust domination systems. He did not make honesty optional when the truth struck him as inconvenient. And he *never* aligned himself with brute, dishonest power to guarantee his own success. So here is the question the historical Jesus as the Christ of faith raises for us today: can we, as Dietrich Bonhoeffer did on his way to the gallows for the "crime" of confronting the untruth of Adolf Hitler, stand for the Truth as Jesus—and Bonhoeffer—did? Can we *belong* to the Truth?

As the church year rolls into Advent, a season of waiting, longing, and listening, faithful followers of the Jesus Way will walk into the expectant darkness, waiting for the light to dawn, for the Truth to reveal itself, for the first cries of a vulnerable baby to redefine kingship, authority, and power. Of course, there are good reasons to fear the erosion of truth. But people of faith are not a people bereft of hope. Truth will survive against all odds.

— 20 —

An Epilogue in Process

Mark 6:1–13

One of the lessons I learned from Mircea Eliade, who was one of the founding "fathers" of the academic discipline known as "History of Religions," is the ubiquitous power of myths. Myths are origin stories human beings tell themselves and periodically reenact through rituals. Reenacting an origin story symbolically places us in sacred times and places more creative and real than the present times and places we inhabit. That is, myths are origin stories about how something real broke into the universe for the very first time in a particular place. Origin times and places are more real than our present times and places; and the further away we are from a time and place of origins, the less real our time and place become. So liturgically reenacting an origin story brings the reality of that Sacred time and place into our own time and place. For example, this is what happens every time Christians celebrate the Eucharist. Every time we eat bread and drink wine as the pastor intones, "This is my body, broken for you" and "This is my blood of the New Covenant shed for you and all creation," we at that moment share Jesus' last supper with his disciples "on the night in which he was betrayed." Myths, "origin stories," dictate the things we believe, the brands we buy, the holidays we celebrate, and the people we revere or despise.

Having been raised by parents who fought through the Great Depression and the Second World War, I was steeped in origin stories—stories about my grandfather's and grandmother's move

AN EPILOGUE IN PROCESS

from Nebraska to Missouri to Arkansas and then west to the plains of Colorado, failing in three farms until my grandfather became a cabinet maker in Pueblo, Colorado, where I was born in 1939. At family gatherings, stories were tole, the same stories year after year, about where my family came from and where they were now. "Work hard, get an education, be honest in the process, and your life will be successful, was the mantra my brothers and cousins were told over and over again. "It's the only way to get out of the poverty we went through," my parents instructed. My father was the only one of his three brothers to graduate from high school, and one of the disappointments of his life was he didn't have the financial resources to attend college even though he graduated at the top of his class at Pueblo High School in 1936. "Above all," he said, "remember where you came from, so you don't get stuck there."

Truth be told, I liked embracing my family's origin stories because through them I enjoyed deep, multigenerational family ties. But when these same origin stories dictated who my friends could be—sorry, no African Americans, Mexicans, or Japanese allowed—they ceased to be life-giving. So as my origin stories gave me a sense of where I came from, who I am, and who I might become, they also dictated who my friends could be and which racial and ethnic groups I needed to distrust. And I felt my origin story's power to oppress and suffocate me.

I suspect that this is why Mark 6:1-13 is so meaningful to me. A far as I can remember, I was introduced to this text by my New Testament instructor when I was an undergraduate at Chapman University in 1957—a story about the time Jesus returned to Nazareth, his home town, after a wildly successful prophetic debut. In the weeks preceding his return he earned a reputation for his wisdom. He proclaimed God's kingdom in provocative parables. He surrounded himself with twelve loyal disciples. He exorcised demons, healed the sick, calmed a storm, and raised a young girl from the dead. In other words, he was a hometown boy who made good. Or so one would like to think. According to Mark, when Jesus entered the synagogue of his boyhood and began to teach, things at first go very well. But after a while, he is received with astonishment and curiosity: "Where did this man get all this? What is this wisdom that has been given to him? What deeds of power are being done by his hands!"

Then someone in the crowd pulls out an old origin story and starts circulating it around the synagogue: "Is not this the carpenter, the son of Mary and brother of James and Joses and Judas and Simon? Are not his sisters here among us?" And they took offense at him, because the only reason to identify someone by his mother in the patriarchal society of Jesus's day was to question his legitimacy. In other words, to refer to Jesus as "the son of Mary" (and not, "the son of Joseph") was a calculated act, a weaponized use of Jesus's origin story to shame him into silence. In a social system where one's status was fixed at birth, it was not considered possible for someone like Jesus—a mere carpenter of questionable parentage—to amount to anything. In other words, he had no business rising above his dicey beginnings, no cultural permission to outgrow his origin story.

The truly sad thing about this story is that the townspeople's suspicion and resentment diminished Jesus's ability to work good on their behalf. "He could do no deeds of power there," Mark writes with grim finality. In some mysterious and disturbing way, the people's small-mindedness, their lack of trust, and their inability to embrace a new facet of Jesus's life and mission, kept them in spiritual poverty. They were unable to welcome the unfamiliar within the familiar. They were uninterested in glimpsing the extraordinary within the ordinary. They couldn't imagine a newer and roomier story when the old one was so juicy. And in the process, they missed the presence of God in their midst.

As I reflected on this story, and still reflect, I could not help but wonder how, when, and where *I* misuse origin stories—my own or other people's—to limit God's actions in the world. How do I refuse to let others in my life grow and change? When do I box them into stories that are unfairly narrow and constricting? Where in my life did I take offense at the new and the unfamiliar, instead of being opened by curiosity and delight? Did I allow the people with whom I am close to *become*? Did I allow *myself* to become?

Or did I cut myself and others off with burdensome narratives none of us can bear: You will *always* be . . . small, weak, broken, insufficient, disappointing. You will *never* outgrow . . . your background, race, family, upbringing, wounds, addictions.

Spiritual maturation requires untangling these stories, sorting fact from fiction (or, more precisely, truth from untruth), and embracing those stories that move us toward wholeness while rejecting or reinterpreting those that do harm. This is not easy. It takes patience and humility, and sometimes it hurts a great deal. In my late seventies, I am still untangling the origin stories I grew up with, trying to let go of the parts that weaken and diminish me, while trying fresh ways to embrace the parts that resonate with my experiences.

The disconcerting truth about this account about Jesus's visit to his home town is that we—the Church—are the modern-day equivalents of Jesus's ancient townspeople. Once we leave home we can never return. Yet church people are the ones who think they know Jesus best. The ones jaded by religious over-familiarity. The ones who take offense when Jesus shows up anew. What will it take to follow him into new and uncomfortable territory? To see him where we least desire to look?

Jesus was a lowly peasant carpenter. Jesus was the one with the tainted birth story. Jesus was the brother of, the son of, the friend of, the neighbor of. We might be scandalized by Jesus's humble origins, but God is not. We might amaze God with our unbelief, but God will call out to us nevertheless, daring us always to see and experience God anew. Maybe, *"Remember who you are and where you come from,"* is God's best reminder to us. We are God's children and the scandal of the Incarnation is precisely that Jesus is the hometown boy made good, an origin story we can never outgrow.

Bibliography

Anatolios, Khaled, ed. *Athanasius*. Early Church Fathers. London: Routledge, 2004, 75–6.
Armstrong, Karen. *The Spiritual Staircase: My Climb Out of Darkness*. New York: Knopf, 2004.
Berger, Peter. *The Heretical Imperative: Contemporary Possibilities of Religious Affirmation*. Garden City, NY: Doubleday, 1979.
Boltz-Weber, Nadia. *Accidental Saints: Finding God in All the Wrong People*. New York: Convergent, 2015.
Bonhoeffer, Deitrich. *The Cost of Discipleship*. 2nd rev. ed. New York: Macmillan,1995.
Borg, Marcus J. *The Heart of Christianity: Rediscovering a Life of Faith*. New York: HarperOne, 2003.
———. *Jesus: Uncovering the Life, Teachings, and Relevance of a Religious Revolutionary*. New York: HarperOne, 2006.
———. *Meeting Jesus Again for the First Time: The Historical Jesus and the Heart of Contemporary Faith*. San Francisco: HarperSanFrancisco, 1994.
Cobb, John B., Jr. *Jesus as Abba: The God Who Has not Failed*. Minneapolis: Fortress, 2015.
———. *Christ in a Pluralistic Age*. 1975. Reprint, Eugene, OR: Wipf & Stock, 1999.
———. *Theological Reminiscences*. Claremont, CA: Process Century Press, 2014.
Crossan, John Dominic. *The Historical Jesus: The Life of a Mediterranean Jewish Peasant*. San Francisco: Harper, 1991.
Dillard, Anne. *Pilgrim at Tinker's Creek*. New York: Harper & Row, 1985.
———. *Teaching a Stone to Talk: Expeditions and Encounters*. New York: Harper & Row, 1982.
Dunne, John S. *The Way of All the Earth: Experiments in Truth and Religion*. Notre Dame: University of Notre Dame Press, 1978.
Eisley, Loren. "The Hidden Teacher." In *The Unexpected Universe*, 48–66. New York: Harcourt, 1969.

Elie, Paul. *The Life You Save May Be Your Own: An American Pilgrimage.* New York: Farrar, Straus, & Giroux, 2003.
Hanson, K. C., and Douglas E. Oakman. *Palestine in the Time of Jesus: Social Structures and Social Conflicts.* 2nd ed. Minneapolis: Fortress, 2008.
Hedges, Chris. *Empire of Illusion: The End of Literacy and the Triumph of Spectacle.* New York: Nation Books, 2009.
Hick, John A. *A Christian Theology of Religions: The Rainbow of Faiths.* Louisville: Westminster John Knox, 1995.
———. *God Has Many Names.* Philadelphia: Westminster, 1982.
———. *An Interpretation of Religion: Human Responses to the Transcendent.* New Haven: Yale University Press, 1989.
———. "The Non-Absoluteness of Christianity." In *The Myth of Christian Uniqueness: Toward a Pluralistic Theology of Religions,* edited by John Hick and Paul F. Knitter, 16–36. Faith Meets Faith. 1987. Reprint, Eugene, OR: Wipf & Stock, 2005.
Ingram, Paul O. *Theological Reflections at the Boundaries.* Eugene, OR: Cascade Books, 2012.
———. *Wrestling with God.* Eugene, OR: Cascade Books, 2006.
———. *Wrestling with the Ox: A Theology of Religious Experience.* 1997. Reprint, Eugene, Or: Wipf & Stock, 2006.
Keating, John P. *Open Mind, Open Heart: The Contemplative Dimension of the Gospel.* New York: Continuum, 1997.
Keller, Catherine. *Cloud of the Impossible: Negative Theology and Planetary Entanglement.* Insurrection: Critical Studies in Religion, Politics, and Culture. New York: Columbia University Press, 2014.
Niebuhr, H. Richard. *The Meaning of Revelation.* Library of Theological Ethics. Louisville: Westminster John Knox, 2006.
Norris, Kathleen. *Amazing Grace: A Vocabulary of Faith.* New York: Riverhead, 1998.
———. *The Cloister Walk.* New York: Riverhead, 1996.
Oakman, Douglas E. *Jesus and the Peasants.* Matrix 4. Eugene, OR: Cascade Books, 2008.
———. *The Political Aims of Jesus.* Minneapolis: Fortress, 2012.
Polkinghorne, John. *The Faith of a Physicist: Reflections of a Bottom-Up Thinker.* Minneapolis: Fortress, 1996.
Schillebeeckx, Edward. *The Church: The Human Story of God.* Translated by John Bowden. New York: Crossroads, 1990.
Sells, Michael. *The Mystical Languages of Unsaying.* Chicago: University of Chicago Press, 1994.
Smith, Wilfred Cantwell. *Belief in History.* Richard Lectures for 1974–75, University of Virginia. Charlottesville: University of Virginia Press, 1977.
———. *Faith and Belief.* Princeton: Princeton University Press, 1979.
———. *The Faith of Other Men.* New York: New American Library, 1963.
———. *The Meaning and End of Religion.* Minneapolis: Fortress, 1991.

BIBLIOGRAPHY

Tillich, Paul. *Systematic Theology*. Vol. 1, *Reason and Revelation, Being and God*. Chicago: University of Chicago Press, 1951.

Toynbee, Arnold. "What Should be the Christian Approach to Contemporary Non-Christian Faith?" In *Christianity among the Religions of the World*, 83–112. Hewitt Lectures, 1956. New York: Scribner, 1957.

Whitehead, Alfred North. *Process and Reality: An Essay in Cosmology*. Corrected ed. Edited by David Ray Griffin and Donald W. Sherburne. New York: Free Press, 1985.

Wright, N. T. *The Day the Revolution Began: Reconsidering the Meaning of Jesus's Crucifixion*. New York: HarperOne, 2016.